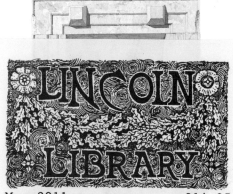

THE GREEK ISLANDS

Genius Loci

View of Naxos island seen through the monumental doorway of the Archaic temple.
Thomas Hope (1769-1831)   Watercolour, 44 x 29 cm.   Benaki Museum, Inv. No. 27375.

Author's acknowledgements

This series of twenty books covering the Aegean Islands is the fruit of many years of solitary dedication to a job difficult to accomplish given the extent of the subject matter and the geography involved. My belief throughout has been that only what is seen with the eyes can trustfully be written about; and to that end I have attempted to walk, ride, drive, climb, sail and swim these Islands in order to inspect everything talked about here. There will be errors in this text inevitably for which, although working in good faith, I alone am responsible. Notwithstanding, I am confident that these are the best, most clearly explanatory and most comprehensive artistic accounts currently available of this vibrant and historically dense corner of the Mediterranean.

Professor Robin Barber, author of the last, general, *Blue Guide to Greece* (based in turn on Stuart Rossiter's masterful text of the 1960s), has been very generous with support and help; and I am also particularly indebted to Charles Arnold for meticulously researched factual data on the Islands and for his support throughout this project. I could not have asked for a more saintly and helpful editor, corrector and indexer than Judy Tither. Efi Stathopoulou, Peter Cocconi, Marc René de Montalembert, Valentina Ivancich, William Forrester and Geoffrey Cox have all given invaluable help; and I owe a large debt of gratitude to John and Jay Rendall for serial hospitality and encouragement. For companionship on many journeys, I would like to thank a number of dear friends: Graziella Seferiades, Ivan Tabares, Matthew Kidd, Martin Leon, my group of Louisianan friends, and my brother Iain— all of whose different reactions to and passions for Greece have been a constant inspiration.

This work is dedicated with admiration and deep affection to Ivan de Jesus Tabares-Valencia who, though a native of the distant Andes mountains, from the start understood the profound spiritual appeal of the Aegean world.

McGILCHRIST'S GREEK ISLANDS

5. RHODES
WITH SYMI & CHALKI

Nigel McGilchrist

GENIUS LOCI PUBLICATIONS
London

McGilchrist's Greek Islands Rhodes with Symi and Chalki
First edition

Published by Genius Loci Publications
54 Eccleston Road, London W13 0RL

Nigel McGilchrist © 2010
Nigel McGilchrist has asserted his moral rights.

ISBN 978-1-907859-05-2

A CIP catalogue record of this book is available from the British Library.

The author and publisher cannot accept responsibility or liability for
information contained herein, this being in some cases difficult to verify
and subject to change.

Layout and copy-editing by Judy Tither

Cover design by Kate Buckle

Maps and plans by Nick Hill Design

Printed and bound in Great Britain by TJ International Ltd, Padstow, Cornwall

The island maps in this series are based on the cartography of
Terrain Maps
Karneadou 4, 106 75 Athens, Greece
T: +30 210 609 5759, Fx: +30 210 609 5859
terrain@terrainmaps.gr
www.terrainmaps.gr

This book is one of twenty which comprise the complete, detailed
manuscript which the author prepared for the *Blue Guide: Greece,
the Aegean Islands* (2010), and on which the *Blue Guide* was
based. Some of this text therefore appears in the *Blue Guide*.

CONTENTS

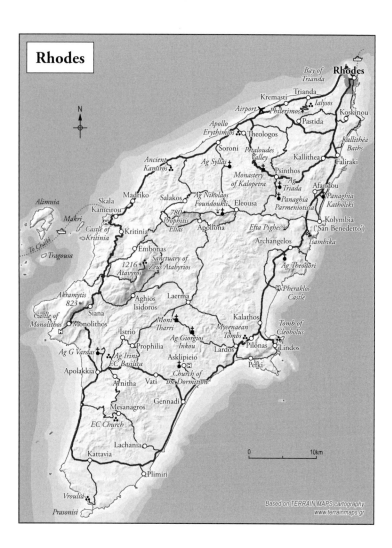

Rhodes

Rhodes

Bay of Trianda

Trianda

Kremasti

Ialysos

Koskinou

Airport

Philerimos

Pastida

Apollo Erythimios

Theologos

Kallithéa Baths

Soroni

Petaloudes Valley

Kallithea

Faliraki

Ancient Kamiros

Ag Syllas

Monastery of Kalopetra

Psinthos

Madriko

Salakos

Ag Nikolaos Foundoukli

Eleousa

Ag Triada

Panaghia Parmeniotissa

Afandou

Panaghia Katholiki

Skala Kameirou

780 Prophitis Elias

Apollona

Efta Pighes

Archangelos

Kolymbia ("San Benedetto")

Makri

Castle of Kritinia

Kritinia

Tsambika

Alimnia

To Chalki

Tragousa

Embonas

Sanctuary of Zeus Atabyrios

1216 Atavyros

Ag Theodori

Pheraklos Castle

Akramytis 823

Aghios Isidoros

Laerma

Kalathos

Tomb of Cleobolus

Castle of Monolithos

Siana

Monolithos

Istrio

Moni Tharri

Mycenaean Tombs

Pilonas

Lindos

Prophilia

Ag Giorgios Inkou

Lardos

Ag G Vardas

Ag Irini EC Basilica

Asklipieio

Pefki

Apolakkia

Arnitha

Vati

Church of the Dormition

Gennadi

Mesanagros

EC Church

Lachania

Kattavia

Plimiri

Vroulia

Prasonisi

0   10km

Based on TERRAIN MAPS cartography
www.terrainmaps.gr

N

RHODES

Cosmopolitan, spacious, immensely varied, blessed with a fullness of vegetation and an unforgettable radiance of light, the island of Rhodes has always been a proudly self-sufficient world of its own. The first line of Horace's seventh Ode cites '*claram Rhodon*' as a paragon of beauty, and the poet's choice of the word *clarus* artfully evokes not only its 'fame' but also the 'brilliance' of its light: the island was, from the beginning, sacred to Helios, divinity of the sun. Roman statesmen and emperors travelled here to enjoy and imbibe the island's art and culture, and intellectuals from all over the civilised world came to study with its scientists, thinkers and orators.

The island has a long and important history. One of its most fascinating moments relates to the creation of the city of Rhodes itself. It is a testimony to the pragmatism and (intermittent) farsightedness of the Ancient Greek mind that three, well-established, thriving and competing ancient cities in different parts of the island—*Lindos, Ialysos* and *Kameiros*—should have taken the peaceful and momentous decision to '*synoecise*' in 408/7 BC—that is, to renounce their individual independence and combine together so as to found and build a new and greater city which was to be called, like the island, 'Rhodes'. This phenomenon had happened elsewhere in the Greek world but rarely on such a significant scale. Each city knew that what it was combining to create would eclipse its own individual importance: but the result was the emergence of one of the richest cities of the later Greek world, extravagantly praised by Strabo and Pliny for its beauty and wealth of art.

Out of the blue, over a thousand years later, the island's character was once again utterly transformed, this time by the arrival of an international group of wealthy, aristocratic warriors—the Hospitaller Knights of St John—who embellished and cultivated and fortified the island as a chivalric kingdom in the sea. The Knights too were a kind of *synoecism*—an unique confluence of different nationalities with common Christian interests, creating something that was not a state, nor a nation, nor anything that had a precedent, but which was nonetheless a fully independent entity and which became a crucial—sometimes solitary—player in the theatre of Mediterranean history. Finally, at the beginning of the last century, the Italians arrived with different ambitions and built Rhodes into a regional capital of their empire with a new centre created in a memorable, but somewhat alien and eclectic kind of architecture. In short, there is nothing commonplace in the story of this remarkable island.

As a consequence, of all the cities in Greece Rhodes is the only one that comes close to Athens in the density and richness of its monuments. In fact, in the sheer variety to be seen—Hellenistic, Mediaeval, Ottoman, Traditional, Italian Colonial—it substantially outshines the capital. Modern Rhodes lives naturally and unaffectedly with this legacy. Although it has more than its fair share of heavy tourism the island does not live solely on its past but supports a vital and independent commercial and cultural life of its own which makes it an equal pleasure to visit in or out of season. An acquaintance with the island takes time; but it will continue to surprise with new finds however often visited. The interest of the city itself is amply matched by the island as a whole where there is an exhilarating array of monuments which, in one way or another, are out of the ordinary. Amongst ancient archaeological sites in the Islands, Ancient *Kameiros* is one of the most untouched having suffered no over-building or interference between its abandonment at the end of Antiquity and its re-discovery at the beginning of the last century. Few sanctuaries in all of Greece have a more improbable or panoramic site than that of Zeus *Atabyrios* on the summit of the island's highest peak. Three of the most complete painted Byzantine interiors in the Aegean—each quite distinct from the other—are to be seen in the main churches at

Lindos, Asklepieío, and at the Monastery of Tharri; and for the quality and idiosyncrasy of their artists' style, the murals in the much smaller churches of Aghii Giorgios and Michaïl at Prophilía (12th century), and of Aghios Nikolaos at Trianda (15th century) should not be missed. Dozens more chapels with painted interiors dot the intimate and bucolic landscape of the island's interior: one of particular charm, the rural chapel of Aghios Nikolaos 'Foundoukli', lies just outside the island's most bizarre village—the semi-abandoned Italian agricultural settlement, now called Eleoúsa on the slopes of Mount Prophitis Elias, whose buildings in an eclectic architecture of the 1930s are now mostly derelict. The folded hills of the deserted centre of the island and the dunes of its south are home to many unusual trees, flowers, reptiles, birds and butterflies. The only European home of the *Liquidambar orientalis* tree, with its curative and calmative gum and beautiful autumn colours, is on Rhodes; its presence is part of the reason for the extraordinary display of the millions of Jersey tiger moths that congregate nearby in the 'Petaloudes Valley' in high summer. There are wild peonies that grow in the lower mountain slopes; and turtles in the shallow waters of the south. All of them are a rare beauty to behold; but their continued presence on the island cannot for ever be taken for granted.

HISTORY AND LEGEND.

The name of the island is often said to derive from the Greek word for a rose, '*rhodon*', but may more probably come from the Phoenician word '*erod*' meaning 'a snake'. In ancient literature the island is referred to by several names, amongst them: *Ophiousa* (deriving again from its snakes), *Aithrea*, *Telchinia* etc. Our most ample source for the legend of the island's origin is Pindar's *Seventh Olympian Ode*—written for Diagoras of Rhodes, the Olympic victor of 464 BC—which tells of the birth of Rhodes, daughter of Aphrodite and bride of Helios, the Sun God. Camirus, Ialysus and Lindus, the eponymous heroes of the island's three principal cities, were their offspring.

Earliest Antiquity to Hellenistic times

Earliest finds, from the Neolithic period (especially from the area of Trianda), show that the island was under the influence of Minoan and subsequently of Mycenaean culture. Rhodes suffered considerably from the eruption of Thera in the late 17th century BC: substantial deposits of volcanic ash from the eruption have been found at a considerable depth on the northwest of the island. Already in Homer the three main cities of Rhodes are mentioned—

Lindos, Ialysos and *Kameiros* (*Iliad*, II, 656). Together with *Cos, Cnidos* and *Halicarnassus*, they formed the 'Dorian Hexapolis' of the southwest corner of Asia Minor. Together they established trade routes throughout the Mediterranean and founded colonies in the neighbouring islands and on the coasts of Asia Minor and Europe; *Gela* in Sicily, founded by *Lindos*, was one of the most significant of these. *Lindos* also participated in the 7th century founding of the enclave of *Naucratis* in Egypt; and mercenaries from the island fought for the Pharaohs on several occasions. In the 6th century BC the island's cities were governed by tyrants. Rhodes submitted to the Persian invaders in 490 BC; but after the victory of the Greeks, it was co-opted into the Delian Confederacy in 478 BC as a subject-ally of Athens. In 412/11 BC, however, the Rhodians revolted in favour of Sparta, late in the Peloponnesian War.

The most decisive moment in the island's ancient history was the *synoecism* of 408/7, in which the three cities of *Ialysos, Kameiros* and *Lindos* peacefully united to found jointly and on equal terms the new federal city of '*Rhodes*' which they populated with their own citizens. Strabo says that it was Hippodamus of Miletus, the most famous town-planner of Antiquity, who laid out the new city beside the group of fine natural harbours at the northern point of the island. The city soon became prosperous and prominent. At first it had an oligarchic government and remained largely loyal to Sparta, but in 395 BC a pro-Athenian faction gained supremacy and the citizens joined cause with the Athenians in defeating the Spartans at the battle of Cnidos in 394 BC. A democratic constitution was then adopted, and in 378 BC Rhodes joined the Second Athenian Confederacy. In 357 BC at the instigation of Mausolus, king of Caria, the island revolted against Athens once again. In 332 BC a Macedonian garrison was briefly (and unpopularly) installed but was expelled shortly after. In the succession wars that followed the death of Alexander the Great, the Rhodians allied themselves closely with Ptolemy I who crucially assisted them in 305/4 BC when their city was besieged by Demetrius Poliorcetes. (The Rhodians afterwards accorded divine honours to Ptolemy as their saviour—hence his epithet 'Soter'.) Demetrius was (somewhat unusually for him) compelled to raise the siege after a year, and it is said that he was so impressed by the islanders' valour that he left them most of his siege artillery, the proceeds from the sale of which they put towards the cost of dedicating a 32m high (105ft) bronze statue of Helios, the island's patron divinity. The statue, later known as the Colossus of Rhodes, was shaken down by an earthquake in 227 BC and never re-erected.

Because of its strategic position, Rhodes developed into an important centre of trade between Italy, Greece, Macedonia, Asia and Africa. It also became the principal naval power of the Aegean. Rhodian law, the earliest code of maritime law, was widely accepted and respected: Augustus and Justinian were both later to adopt it as a model, and a number of its provisions are still cited today. With a population of 60,000–80,000, the city was lavishly adorned and it enjoyed an artistic golden age. Pliny claimed that the city had no fewer than 2,000 statues, many of them colossal. The great earthquake of 227 BC wrought widespread devastation, but it subsequently inspired an international programme of aid in money and talent. In its heyday the island became a beacon of civilisation: the orator Aeschines (c. 397–c. 322 BC), after his discomfiture at the hands of Demosthenes, founded at Rhodes a school of rhetoric which was later to be attended by many distinguished Romans—among them Cato, Cicero, Julius Caesar, and Lucretius. The 3rd century BC Alexandrian poet, Apollonius, taught rhetoric at Rhodes with so much success that the Rhodians honoured him with the cognomen *'Rhodius'*.

Roman, Early Christian and Byzantine times

As the Roman presence and power grew in the Aegean, Rhodes—which was rich and now, to a large degree, independent—was much divided between pro- and anti-Roman factions. The island helped Rome both in its struggle against Philip V of Macedon, leading to the defeat of the latter at Cynoscephalae in Thessaly in 197 BC, and in its war against Antiochus (III) the Great, king of Syria in 188 BC, and gained control of the Cyclades as a result of the first, and of territory in Caria and Lycia, adjacent to the island's large and important *peraea* of dependent settlements, after the second. But Rhodes's equivocation in the Third Macedonian War brought swift Roman retribution: after the Battle of Pydna in 168 BC, she had to surrender her possessions on the mainland of Asia Minor. Two years later, her commercial supremacy ended when the Romans declared Delos a free port. In the Mithridatic wars, the island recovered some favour with Rome and successfully resisted Mithridates' siege of the city. Sulla restored to Rhodes some of her former possessions in Asia

Minor; but the island sided with Julius Caesar in the civil war and suffered in consequence at the hands of Cassius, who plundered the city in 43 BC and captured the Rhodian fleet, effectively terminating the island's naval power and self-sufficiency. Augustus accorded to Rhodes the title of 'Allied City'; Vespasian incorporated the island into the Roman Province of Asia; and under Diocletian (284–305 AD) Rhodes became the capital of the 'Province of the Islands'.

St Paul briefly visited Rhodes in 60 AD, allegedly landing at Lindos (*Acts*, XXI, 1). The island appears to have had its own bishop from a very early date, who was among those who participated in the first church council in Nicaea in 325 AD. In 1274 a Metropolitan of Rhodes attended the Council of Lyons and appears as a signatory of the short-lived reunion of the Eastern and Latin churches.

For Byzantium, Rhodes represented an important base for the navy it deployed against Arab expansion; but its defence was often deficient, and after 654 the island was frequently pillaged, and for a time occupied, by Saracens. Already by 1082, though, the Venetians had negotiated with Emperor Alexander Comnenus a presence on the island with significant privileges. Rhodes was also an important staging post for troops and pilgrims on the way to the Holy Land. During the Fourth Crusade, which established the Latin empire of Constantinople, Rhodes was taken over by the scion of a Byzantine naval family, Leo Gavalas, who declared the independence of the island. Within half a century the Genoese, however, were in partial control of Rhodes, and it was they, in the person of Vignolo de' Vignoli, who came to an agreement with the refugee Knights of St John of Jerusalem jointly to invade and occupy the island.

Under the Knights of St John

The origin of the Order of the Knights of St John goes back to the foundation in 1048 of a hospital in Jerusalem, built by merchants from Amalfi for the benefit and protection of pilgrims travelling to visit the Holy Sepulchre. Their first rector, Gérard, formed the Knights into a strictly constituted religious body subject to the jurisdiction of the Patriarch of Jerusalem; but it was not long before the Order became predominantly military and the Knights were sworn to defend the Holy Sepulchre to the death and to make war on infidels wherever they were to be found. In 1191 Saladin captured Jerusalem and the Knights were evicted. They retreated to Acre, from which they were expelled a century later after a terrible siege. In 1291 they sailed to Cyprus. The period was further marred by a bitter and unresolved animosity between the Knights Hospitaller and the Knights Templar, which ended in hostilities in which the Templars prevailed. In 1306 the Hospitallers were again compelled to flee from Cyprus to Rhodes. Having in vain demanded the fief of Rhodes from the Emperor in Byzantium, they then took the island by force in 1309, after more than two years' siege. Their possession of it was recognised and supported by the Pope.

There were three 'horizontal' levels or classes within the Order—knights (*milites*), chaplains (*cappelani*), and serving brothers or fighting squires (*servientes armorum*) who followed the knights into action; and seven 'vertical' divisions according to nationality—Provence, Auvergne, France, Italy, Spain (later, in 1461, subdivided into Aragon and Castile), England and Germany. These were called *Langues* or 'Tongues'. Each 'Tongue' had a Bailiff, and its own headquarters or *Auberge*. The Bailiffs, under the presidency of the Grand Master who was elected for life by the Knights, formed the chapter of the Order. The modern British Order of St John of Jerusalem, founded in 1827, is effectively a later revival of the 'Tongue' of England.

The plan which the Knights had for Rhodes was clear and far-sighted. They set out to re-fortify the city with a thoroughness which few other cities in the world had seen, and in a way that responded to the rapidly changing realities of warfare. They were to fortify the island itself with castles, and then to further fortify the surrounding islands to the north, west and east, so as to create an impregnable 'navy' of islands, subordinate to the 'flagship' of Rhodes, riding at anchor off the coast of Turkey. They also built a powerful marine fleet which protected the island's trade. For two fraught centuries the Knights of St John defied the Turks. They took part in the capture and later in the defence of Smyrna; and in Rhodes they withstood two great sieges—in 1444 by the Sultan of Egypt, and in 1480 by Mehmet the Conqueror. During the latter, their 'Turcopolier', or Commander of Light Cavalry, was an Englishman, John Kendal. As soon as Mehmet lifted his siege, the Knights set immediately about fortifying the city once again in new and ever-more ingenious ways. At last, in June 1522, Sultan Suleiman the Magnificent, having captured Belgrade, turned his attention to Rhodes and attacked the city with a force said to have numbered 100,000 men. The Knights mustered only 650, with the addition of

200 Genoese sailors, 50 Venetians, 400 Cretans and 600–800 other inhabitants of the city. Pope Adrian VI implored the Christian princes in vain to come to their aid. The Turks blockaded the city by sea, and eventually secured the heights above it, from which they pounded the fortifications with artillery. The besieged constantly repaired the breaches in their walls: their sophisticated defences would probably have been able to endure and even outlast the Sultan's siege. But it was human frailty instead, that was the defenders' undoing—exhaustion, diminishing numbers, and the actions of traitors. The siege was over by Christmas of 1522, and the Sultan allowed the Knights to capitulate on honourable terms, permitting them to leave the city unhindered within two weeks. On New Years Day 1523, the Grand Master, Villiers de l'Isle Adam, sailed out of Rhodes and led his 180 surviving brethren first to Candia (Herakleion) in Crete and finally, after six years of uncertainty and peregrination, to Malta in 1530. Given the defeat that the Turks would eventually suffer at the hands of the Knights in Malta, Suleiman might well have had reason to rue his magnaminity in Rhodes.

The Ottoman occupation and modern times

For nearly 400 years from 1523 until 1912, Rhodes was a provincial administrative capital of the Ottoman Empire. All churches in the city, from the smallest to the largest, were converted into mosques; and a number of fine, new Islamic religious complexes were erected. The Greeks were ousted from within the walls of the Old Town, which remained inhabited only by the Jews (in the eastern corner) and by the Turkish masters. The Greek population had to resettle in the outlying areas; but many were to emigrate over the subsequent centuries, especially to Egypt. Those who remained enjoyed a period of relative prosperity and stability in the 18th and 19th centuries.

In 1912, during their war with Turkey, the Italians captured Rhodes after a short siege; their possession of the island was only recognised by international treaty (Lausanne) in 1924. The 1920s saw an ambitious programme of building and improvement in infrastructure by the Italians. But their intentions and ambitions became rapidly less benign in the late 1930s with the increasingly restrictive, Fascist policies emanating from Rome. In the latter part of the Second World War the Germans took over from the Italians. In 1945 the island was freed by British and Greek commandos, and in 1947 officially became part of the Greek State.

POSTSCRIPT ON RHODIAN ART

Ancient

The notable prosperity, cosmopolitan culture and rapid expansion of the city of Rhodes after its foundation in 408/7 BC brought an influx of famous artists. Most famous of all was Lysippus of Sicyon, the sculptor attached to the court of Alexander the Great, who created on Rhodes his famous *Four-horse Chariot of the Sun*. A 'School of Rhodes' flourished under his influence, later much lauded by Pliny (*Nat. Hist.*, XXXIV). It included Protogenes, the painter and protégé of Apelles; Chares of Lindos, creator of the *Colossus of Rhodes* and originator of a long tradition of bronze sculpture in the city; Bryaxis, who worked on the *Mausoleum* of Halicarnassus; and Philiskos, author of a group of the *Muses*, which was later carried off to Rome, perhaps by Crassus, and placed in the Porticus of Octavia. Inspired by Lysippus, Philiskos was especially skilled in the treatment of drapery.

During the Roman ascendancy of the 2nd and 1st centuries BC, artistic activity continued in Rhodes, although it conformed more to the taste and grandeur desired by the new commissioning masters. Rhodian sculptors made a colossal statue, 12m high, dedicated to the Roman people and placed in the Temple of Athena Polias and Zeus Polieus on the Acropolis of Rhodes. Apollonios and Tauriskos of Tralles made the virtuoso group depicting the awful revenge wrought upon Dirce by her stepsons, today known as the '*Farnese Bull*', which was found in the Baths of Caracalla in Rome and is now in the Archaeological Museum of Naples. The group of *Menelaus and Patroclus*, a fragment of which survives in Rome under the name of the '*Pasquino*', came from Rhodes. Perhaps best known of all is the *Laocoön*, found in 1506 near the Golden House of Nero in Rome; this group was produced in the 1st century BC by the Rhodian sculptors Agesander, Polydorus, and Athenodorus—authors also of an elaborate series of sculptural groups on Homeric themes found in the Grotto of Sperlonga, to the south of Rome.

Byzantine and mediaeval

With the arrival of the Knights of St John, who naturally favoured the styles of their own native countries, the art of Rhodes soon feels the influence of Western styles:

French and Catalan Gothic features predominate in architecture and Italian in painting. Up until around 1480, the Knights depended on local labour which was unfamiliar with the Gothic style, and a certain awkwardness ensues as the artesans try to reconcile the new style with the older Byzantine elements that were familiar to them. After 1480, especially under the aegis of the energetic Grand Master, Pierre d'Aubusson (1476–1503), Western craftsman were more widely employed. The Gothic character of the work remains, but the forms are more harmonious, the execution more delicate, and the decoration more appealing. The style promoted by the Knights remains predominantly austere, as befits a military order; but it is not without some elements of considerable beauty. The door and window-frames of the period are a rich field of study in themselves, and even the simplest carved string-course of a facade can be a thing of beauty.

Ottoman and modern

Many of the Ottoman monuments on the island remarkably have survived, and are now the object of concerted conservation. The sophistication, both decorative and architectural, of two of the 16th century mosques in particular—that of Recep Pasha, and the Suleimaniye—show that architects of considerable talent, probably from the capital, were brought to Rhodes at the beginning of the Turkish occupation. There are also gateways, houses and many finely carved, Ottoman marble water-fountains both in Rhodes and around the island. The prosperity of the last years of the Turkish presence is characterised by the construction of a number of substantial mansions; some are typically Ottoman in design such as that near the church of St George on Menandrou Street, some are purely neoclassical in design and were largely built by the Greek community in the New Town and in the fashionable areas of Trianda, Kremastí, and Koskinou, while yet others are a hybrid of the two styles, such as the imposing Hadji Halil mansion of 1880/90 on Pythagóra Street. Rhodes also has the oldest, surviving Synagogue in Greece dating from 1575.

Ottoman motifs and ideas permeate the decorative arts of the island of the last three centuries—nowhere more than in what is called 'Rhodian' or 'Lindos Ware'. The exquisite ceramic production of the Turkish workshops of Iznik first came to the island with the Ottoman masters in the 16th century. By the 17th century, a gamut of new im-

ages began to supplement the traditional floral designs—
amongst them images of fully rigged ships. These became
popular with Greek traders and mariners, who decorated their houses with large displays of such plates. Even
though much of this production still came from Iznik itself or from Çanakkale, local imitations and variants were
produced, in particular at Lindos.

The island's latest architectural flowering came with the
Italians in the 1920s. The Master Plan for their 'regional
capital' of Rhodes foresaw the restoration of the city of the
Knights to its former glory in such a way that it would be
an appropriate theatrical backdrop to the new, planned,
administrative centre outside the walls to its north. For
this new creation, a group of talented Italian architects—
Florestano di Fausto, Rodolfo Petracco, Armando Bernabiti and Pietro Lombardi—laid out and designed a wide
variety of buildings in an architectural language which
juxtaposed historical references to a Roman and Venetian
and Hospitaller past with some entirely new elements and
forms. The buildings included residences, churches, banks,
theatres, offices, clubs, recreation facilities, an aquarium
and a thermal baths complex. The result is unusual, and
never monotonous. Only in the late 1930s, with the rapid

deterioration of the situation in Italy, did the architecture take on a more brutal form, in which former decorative elements were 'purged' from its surfaces—ignominiously ending what was a promising architectural experiment.

The guide to the island has been divided into seven sections:-
- *Rhodes: the Old Town—the walls and within*
  a. Northern Sector: the 'Collachium' area, north of Sokrátous Street
  b. Central Sector: south of Sokrátous Street and west of Pythagóra Street
  c. Eastern Sector: east of Pythagóra Street
- *Rhodes: the New Town and areas outside the walls*
- *The northwest of the island and Kameiros*
- *The northeast of the island*
- *Lindos*
- *Central Rhodes and the three mountains*
- *Southern Rhodes*

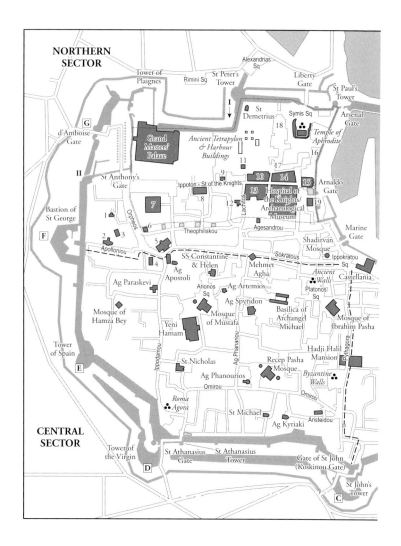

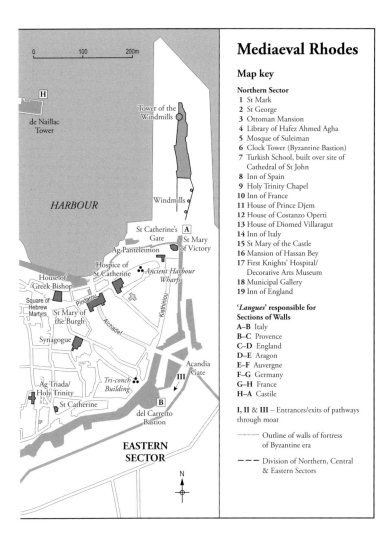

Mediaeval Rhodes

Map key

Northern Sector
1 St Mark
2 St George
3 Ottoman Mansion
4 Library of Hafez Ahmed Agha
5 Mosque of Suleiman
6 Clock Tower (Byzantine Bastion)
7 Turkish School, built over site of Cathedral of St John
8 Inn of Spain
9 Holy Trinity Chapel
10 Inn of France
11 House of Prince Djem
12 House of Costanzo Operti
13 House of Diomed Villaragut
14 Inn of Italy
15 St Mary of the Castle
16 Mansion of Hassan Bey
17 First Knights' Hospital/ Decorative Arts Museum
18 Municipal Gallery
19 Inn of England

'Langues' responsible for Sections of Walls
A–B Italy
B–C Provence
C–D England
D–E Aragon
E–F Auvergne
F–G Germany
G–H France
H–A Castile

I, II & III – Entrances/exits of pathways through moat

⋯⋯⋯ Outline of walls of fortress of Byzantine era

– – – Division of Northern, Central & Eastern Sectors

RHODES: THE OLD TOWN—THE WALLS AND WITHIN

The itineraries below divide the old town into three areas: northern, central and eastern (see map on pp. 28–29).

Churches and their saints have been given Latinate names where they relate to foundations or examples principally of the Hospitaller period. In some cases, however, Greek names have been kept for those saints who are more familiar through the Orthodox tradition.

NORTHERN SECTOR: THE 'COLLACHIUM' AREA, NORTH OF SOKRATOUS STREET

There is no more majestic way to enter the walled, mediaeval town of the Knights of St John than through the magnificent *d'Amboise Gate (1512) in the northwest corner of the city, directly below the Palace of the Grand Master. Forbidding to the stranger and reassuring to the inhabitant, it is the finest of the landward entrances to the city—seen at its most impressive by night. About 200 paces separate the outer approach from the fourth and final inner gate, a distance that was originally punctuated by three drawbridges, a double-bend within the thickness of the first bastion, an independent advance wall, and three dry moats: most of the gates consisted of double sets of doors furthermore. This gives not only an immediate measure of the sophistication and complexity of the city's massive defences, but also of the perceived magnitude of the Turkish threat in the sixteenth century and the seriousness with which Rhodes was considered as the crucial Mediterranean outpost of the Christian West. The design of the walls was a specific response to the nature of the Turkish war machine and to the revolutionary changes that warfare had undergone since the arrival of gunpowder and the invention of cannon. It is important to remember that these fortifications were also the central hub of a further twenty fortresses all over the island and of an extensive network of castles and towers on the other islands in the area, from Kastellorizo in the east as far as Leros in the north. Rhodes was the fortified flagship of a navy of lesser islands riding at anchor off the coast of Asia Minor.

* * * * *

HISTORY AND STRUCTURE OF THE WALLS

*(The walls are best visited after sundown, by taking the
*pathway through the entire length of the moat from Plateia
Alexandrias round to the Acandia Gate. This is open day
and night (free admission) and constitutes a uniquely instructive and evocative walk—especially by moonlight. The
one-hour tour of the top of the walls, from the Grand Master's Palace to the Gate of St John which used to be offered to
the public on Tuesday and Saturday afternoons at 3 pm has
unfortunately been suspended for the moment. For further
information, telephone 22410 23655)*

The topography. The primary importance of the site of
Rhodes town was not—as is often the case elsewhere—the
presence of a good natural acropolis, but rather its group of
natural harbours positioned strategically on the passage of
one of the Mediterranean's most important sea-routes. In
Antiquity the city of Rhodes had such a large population and
extension that it was able to use the summit to the west of
the city (Mount Smith) as an acropolis, and the city's habitation amply filled the space between it and the port. As the
population of the city declined dramatically after the fall of
the Roman Empire, this arrangement became less and less
practicable: the hill was too far from the port. And so an area

was fortified closer to the harbours. Arab chroniclers of the late 7th century refer to such a fortress at Rhodes and archaeology has shown that it existed in the area under, and to the south of, the Palace of the Grand Master. Its ramparts are visible today, to a considerable extent, in Theophiliskou Street. The form of the mediaeval and modern city dates from this fundamental shift in centre of gravity to the area immediately by the port.

The **Byzantine fortress**—to which the whole population would retreat in times of danger, such as in the attacks described by the Arab chroniclers—covered a roughly rectangular area which was later to be called the 'Collachium' by the Knights; it stretched from the commercial harbour up to the Palace of the Grand Master, and was bounded to the north by the line traced by the existing walls and to the south by the ashlar stone ramparts visible in stretches along Theophiliskou and Agesandrou Streets, where some of the regularly spaced towers along these walls are still recognisable. To the south of this fortress area, and at a later date (most probably in the 11th or 12th century), more walls were added to enclose a lower residential and commercial town. These stretched as far south as Omírou Street, and were bounded to the west by the approximate line of Ippodámou Street; to the east they are still clearly visible in excavations near to Pythagóra Street and below ground level to the north of the Mosque of Ibrahim Pasha. These walls were substantial enough to resist the siege by the Knights of St John on their arrival in Rhodes in 1306 for over two years. Until the city fell to them in August of 1309, the Knights were based at Philerimos, 10km to the southwest of the city (*see below*).

The need for change. These Byzantine fortifications belonged to a world of warfare which was suddenly outmoded by a revolution in military technology in the 15th century, namely the arrival of gunpowder and cannon. The amazing speed and success of the invasion of Italy by Charles VIII of France, using yet more accurate cannon-balls made of iron, showed that the traditional premises of mediaeval defence and fortification were obsolete. The ongoing project embarked on by the Knights of St John to re-equip the city and harbours of Rhodes for the new realities of war reflected these fundamental changes. In the last phase, Italian engineers who had become acknowledged experts in ballistics and fortifications after their experience of the French invasion were employed, and the Knights became their most innovative clients. The result is what we see today—one of the most impressive and best-preserved fortified settlements in Europe.

The new enceinte of walls projected by the Knights now

totalled nearly 4km in length. In 1465, to facilitate the onerous undertaking of its fortification, the Order divided its length into eight sectors, each designated to a different nationality or 'Langue' ('Tongue') of Knights within the Order (*see plan on pp. 28–29*). These became the battle-stations of the different Tongues who were each responsible for the defence and maintenance of their own sector. The harbour fortifications were assigned to Castile; then, in clockwise direction from the harbour's southeastern corner, came the landward sectors of Italy, Provence, England, Aragon, Auvergne, Germany and France, whose remit encompassed the Master's Palace and finished at the de Naillac tower at the northwestern side of the port. (The positions of England and Aragon were exchanged shortly before the siege of 1522 to the above order, from their original allocations designated by Grand Master Zacosta in 1465).

The existing walls. The current appearance of the fortifications is the result of two principal periods of construction: the first dating from the 14th and early 15th centuries—before the unsuccessful Turkish siege of 1480 and the destructive earthquake of the following year left them in ruins; the second from between 1481 and the second Turkish siege of 1522 under Suleiman the Magnificent. Later Ottoman repairs (and Italian restoration) were extensive, but alterations to the design were hardly made at all; by then the battle-line between Christendom and Islam had shifted far to the west and the Ottoman Empire relied on its naval power to defend its Aegean possessions. During the whole of the second period of the Knights' re-fortification, however, the threat of attack was so constant that the walls could never be taken down so as to be rebuilt to more modern specifications, but had constantly to be modified and added to instead.

Since the city occupied a sloping terrain with no obvious natural defences, the first necessity was to protect the landward side with a wide, dry moat between the walls and the rising ground beyond. A ditch, at first averaging 15m wide and 10m deep, was cut in the early 14th century: this effectively trapped any enemy attempting to scale or mine the walls in a deadly gulley under the fire from the defenders. The stone and earth from the ditch in turn formed the mass of the defensive walls, which were further protected by two important innovations:

- crenellated *fausse-braies*, built out from the base of the curtain walls whose purpose was both to protect their vulnerable lower area from damaging artillery fire and mining, as well as to increase the scope of defenders' fire (this is best seen in the sector of the Tongue of England, between the Gates of St Athanasius and St John, on the south side of the city);

- a chain of square towers, built in front of the walls and independent of them (as if they were miniature fortresses in themselves), which enormously enlarged the field of fire, covering even the walls themselves if these should happen to be overrun. The towers were joined to the walls by removable bridges, and their independence as structures prevented either tower or wall from being brought down by the collapse of the other. This feature of design is less obvious today because part of the modifications undertaken subsequently involved these towers being incorporated into massively strengthened semi-independent bastions instead, which were buttressed against the walls so as better to resist cannon fire.

Miraculously these walls, with their new elements of design, held out against the forces of Mehmet the Conqueror for over four months in 1480 when they laid siege to Rhodes with the heaviest artillery ever yet deployed against a fortified city. After the siege was lifted, an earthquake in the following year did the remaining damage which Mehmet's forces had not been able to inflict. A complete rethink of their design was now in order.

The second phase of building and post-1480 alterations, involved:

- increasing the height of the walls themselves to match

that of the now incorporated towers and substantially enlarging them on their inside: first from about 2.5m to 5.5m, and then later to 12m in thickness.

- adding long slanting parapets which served to deflect missiles, and angled gun-ports—both new elements of design—at the top of the fortifications;

- broadening the moat significantly so as to put greater distance (often over 50m) between the walls and the attacker's artillery and cannon positions. The earth removed from the moat was also used to increase the height of the facing counterscarp and retaining wall on its outer side. This helped to mask the lower areas of the city's walls from fire—in part because the design of early cannon was such that if the barrel was pointed horizontally or below, the ball could lose contact with the charge, thus aborting its propulsion;

- constructing in the middle of this broader moat, long, free-standing advance walls which ran along the axis of the ditch wherever there were long stretches of exposed wall (e.g to the south and southwest). These enabled the defenders to fire on the enemy from all sides, and severely hindered any attempt to undermine the walls. They also concealed from view further batteries behind them.

One of the particular characteristics of the fortifications

of Rhodes is the constantly changing design from one sector to the next, reflecting the different siege-experience of the nationalities entrusted with their construction and of the engineers employed by them. In some cases, there are small variations in the period of construction which, in an age of rapidly changing war technology, counted for a lot. The radical differences in design between, for example, the facetted Bastion of St George of the Tongue of Auvergne, enlarged in 1521/2, and the slightly earlier, cylindrical del Carretto Bastion (c. 1517, Tongue of Italy) are instructive. The latter, which has something of the intimidating appearance of a modern submarine, was designed by Basilio dalla Scuola, engineer to Maximilian I. It is a sophisticated version of the briefly fashionable 'rondel' type of bastion, with unusually angled artillery embrasures both at the rim and the level of the moat floor. But its smart design did not fully prove its worth in the siege; while the improvised, and more traditional-seeming, bulwark of St George did. Its angled front proved crucially more flexible for enfilading. Its design was adopted in Malta, when the Knights once again began their fortification works—this time with the experiences of Rhodes fresh in their memory.

On the harbour-front, by contrast, the defences still consisted of a curtain wall with parapet and virtually no batter. But three forward fortresses had been built to protect the harbour entrance: first, the Tower of Grand Master de Naillac (1396–1421) on the north mole of the Main ('Commercial') Harbour; and subsequently the Tower of the Windmills to the east, and the Tower of St Nicholas to the north of Mandraki Harbour built under Grand Master Zacosta (1461–67). A chain closed the entrance to the main harbour; and sunken rock debris was used to fill and close the narrow entrance to the boatyards of Mandraki harbour.

Specialists in defence methods were brought in secret to Rhodes at the last moment. The famous Venetian engineer, Gabriele Tadini da Martinengo, defied the specific proscription of his city by coming to the aid of the Knights in Rhodes. He perfected a subterranean warning device—a stretched diaphragm which picked up the least sound or movement and set attached bells ringing. This enabled him to locate undermining and to bury the attackers in their own work by digging transverse tunnels across their path.

In the end, it was not any inherent deficiency in the design of these defences, but the treachery of individuals and exhaustion of manpower that delivered the city to the forces of Suleiman the Magnificent in 1522. The city was, for its time, a uniquely well-designed and well-tuned military machine; it was not designed for a warfare of stealth, but of intimidation. To those who visited in the 15th and 16th centuries it must have appeared a wonder of technology. For the visitor today that wonder has mellowed into a more elegiac and aesthetic appeal.

* * * * *

The outer doorway of the **d'Amboise Gate**, set between two forbidding semicircular bastions, is surmounted by a **marble relief** bearing its date of completion, 1512, below the armorial bearings of its builder, Grand Master Emery d'Amboise (1503–12) which, together with the arms of the Order, are held by an angel while Christ the King blesses from a nimbus above. A wide vaulted passage leads through the thickness of the outer walls and bastion, crosses a second bridge and turns onto a shaded, free-standing advance rampart with moats to either side, towered over by the west face of the Grand Master's Palace to the left. The last of the four sets of gates that comprise this entry into the city is the **Gate of St Anthony**. Above it is a damaged relief sculpture of the saint in red trachitic stone, which has the appearance of porphyry from a distance. To the right of the gate as you approach, steps lead down into an enclosed area littered with large, stone cannon balls. It was against the destructive force of these flying, sculpted boulders that the walls had to resist: some of them measure more than 50cm in diameter and weigh upward of 160kg. Opposite the foot of the steps, in the far corner is a **postern-gate** in the form of a vaulted tunnel which leads into the outer moat underneath the second enceinte of walls. The exterior entrance to this was originally protected from view by a wall which has since been demolished and whose foundations only are visible. The passage enabled the defenders to make surprise sallies against the enemy and to clear debris from the moat which might be used by attackers to fill it. The three shafts which pierce the ceiling of the tunnel could function both for supplying munitions when it was in the possession of the defenders and for attacking intruders if the passageway fell into the hands of the enemy, at which point the tunnel functioned as a trap.

The gate of St Anthony leads into **Orphéos Street**, a lively thoroughfare which cuts through one of the most interesting and varied corners of the city. It is bordered to the right by shops and to the left by the line of the Byzantine walls of the city; further to the left is the Grand Master's Palace and beyond it the Street of the Knights. Ahead lie a number of important Ottoman monuments—the Mosque of Suleiman the Magnificent, the Islamic Library and the Turkish School; and to the right, between the fortifications and Orphéos Street, and bounded by Apollon-íou Street and the Bastion of St George to the south, is a

collection of buildings and excavations which vividly en-
capsulate the historical variety and layered density of the
city. These are best reached by taking the second narrow
entrance to the right which leads into a loop formed by
Ierokléous and Menándrou Streets. A few metres down
Menándrou Street on the right is the 14th century **church
of St Mark**. The Holy Icon of Philerimos was placed here
for a period during the siege of 1522 and survived un-
scathed when the western projection of the church was
destroyed in the bombardment. When the Turks later came to construct a new wall to close the damaged
church on its western side and to convert it into a small
mosque ('Satri Çelebi Mescid'), tombs were discovered in
the floor. In order not to disturb these burials, the floor
was re-filled and a low arch constructed over the area to
support the wall above, obviating the need to dig invasive
foundations. This is visible low down in the west wall.
The church has unequal arms which meet at a vaulted
crossing with no cupola. Two *mihrab* niches are still preserved, and there are vestigial remains of wall-paintings
in the interior.

Just beyond the church is the entrance to the buildings
and garden of the **Marc de Montalembert Foundation**,
created in 1994 to commemorate the life of a young man
of French and Italian parents who died in an accident at

sea, between Rhodes and the Turkish coast. The foundation—whose mission is to further the cause of peace and tolerance, especially among younger people, in the Mediterranean area through grants to projects relating to the history and culture of the region—has recreated a historic garden of remarkable beauty, inspired by and based on the Ottoman gardens formerly on the site, which in turn modified elements from the preceding gardens of Hospitaller and Byzantine Rhodes. The predominantly 'white' garden includes both geometric and informal areas and water elements from the original Ottoman design. (The garden can be partially seen from above when making the tour of the City Walls; otherwise it may be visited by appointment at www.montalembert@fondationmdm.com)

The late 18th century **Ottoman mansion**, to which the garden formerly belonged, is the adjacent building to the south: it has recently undergone extensive restoration. With its unique combination of Ottoman and Hospitaller architectural elements in wood and stone, it constitutes one of the finest examples of its kind in the city. The main southern *selamlık* room still conserves a carved and painted wooden ceiling. The mansion and the garden occupy land which was originally part of the late 14th century *monastery of St George. Some of the monastic outbuildings (now restored) have survived, since the monastery continued to function as the 'Kurmalı Medrese' throughout the Ottoman period. The church itself, of quatrefoil plan, surmounted by an unusually **elongated cupola**, articulated externally by a crown of 20 blind arches decorated with simple cord-line carving, is the most elegant and sophisticated of the 14th century churches of Rhodes. Its plan is similar to the rural church of Aghios Nikolaos Foundoukli near Eleoúsa, in the centre of the island; but St George's perfectly balanced proportions, spacious volumes, graceful lines and fine stonework, have a greater, cosmopolitan sophistication which speaks of an architect of considerable skill and pedigree. It is perhaps the most harmonious church in all of Mediaeval Rhodes. (*Opening times are still to be established by the authorities. From the entrance on Apolloníou Street something of the individuality of the exterior can be appreciated, even when closed.*)

The **interior**, though plain, is luminous and gives an impression of space in excess of its actual size, because of the absence of supporting columns. The floor is in Lardos marble, with inset square and octagonal medallions of *rosso antico* and porphyry. The mouths of earthenware jugs immured in the walls in the corners of the building so as to enhance the acoustics for chant can be seen. In the southeast corner, below the level of the interior, the foundations of the apse of an Early Christian structure have been brought to light; some carved marble fragments from the same period have been placed in the east end of the church—amongst them a fine **marble relief** (? 10th century) depicting the Virgin Mary with hands raised, between her nephew, John the Baptist, and her Son. To its west the church is preceded by a narthex, probably added in the 15th century, entered from the external courtyard through a door surrounded by a **stone cornice carved with running vine-motif**. An area of excavation immediately to the east and northeast of the church has brought to light both the paving and form of a Hellenistic street, as well as the foundations of an **Early Christian basilica**, a large area of whose fine **polychrome marble floor** in *opus sectile* is visible.

Apollôníou Street leads down to the 15th century **bastion of St George**, of the Tongue of Auvergne. This was one of the landward entrances to the city which was prudently closed by Grand Master Pierre d'Aubusson in the interests of greater security in the year before the siege of 1480. In 1521 it was enlarged into a massive bastion which completely encircled the **original square tower** and had an innovative and influential design with angled façades permitting enfilading from all sides. The west face of the original tower displays a fine early 15th century **relief** in Lardos marble of St George killing the dragon.

At the end of Orphéos Street by the junction with Apolloníou is the late 18th century building of the **Hafez Ahmed Agha Library** (*open Mon–Sat 9.30–4. Free admission*), set in a walled courtyard of citrus trees and surrounded on all sides by *chochlakia* (black and white pebble inlay) paving. The library was founded in 1793 as an act of beneficence by one of the Sultan's equerries. It was intended for public use and may once have contained as many as 2,000 Arabic, Persian and Ottoman manuscripts and volumes. The rectangular building is divided into two domed, luminous chambers. A number of Ottoman stone inscriptions have been collected together to the west side of the building.

Directly opposite the library is the handsome **Suleimaniye Mosque**—a faithful early 19th century re-build of the mosque which Suleiman the Magnificent purportedly ordered to be constructed on the site of the Church of the Holy Apostles after his victorious entry into the city in 1523. The building has been brought back from a state of dereliction by the recent consolidation of its structure and ornate minaret, and the restoration of its mostly 18th and 19th century decoration.

The broad design and dynamic roof-scape of rising, shallow domes is typical of 16th century Turkish architecture in the Ottoman capital. The *entrance doorway is particularly fine, and is constructed from the frame and arcosolium of an early 16th century marble monumental tomb of a nobleman. The soffit of the arch above the door is delicately carved with flowers and the sides of the pilasters are decorated with relief depictions of weapons, foliage and ornaments. The doorway is deeply shaded by a long **porch** roofed with small domes and supported on monolithic marble columns which may come from the dismantled Church of the Apostles: the porch is further extended by a wooden veranda. Opposite is the domed *shadirvan*, or ritual fountain.

A mosque of this importance was commonly built along with a complex of other religious and charitable structures. On the corner opposite (southeast) is the mosque's **İmaret** or **Alms-house** (now a café), built around a tranquil courtyard where a few ancient architectural fragments and Ottoman cannon-balls have been collected. The site is believed to be that of the important Hospitaller church dedicated to the Holy Apostles: a cross-vaulted apse belonging to a Gothic structure was recently uncovered behind the baking ovens of the *İmaret* which would appear to belong to the original church.

Raised up on a surviving 7th century **bastion of the original Byzantine walls** to the northwest of the Suleimaniye mosque is the **Clock Tower**, or '*Roloï*', whose eclectic architectural mix has been widely, and perhaps undeservedly, vilified (*open June, July & Aug 9–5, 9–1*). It was erected by Ahmet Fetih Pasha in the year after the gunpowder explosion of 1856 beneath the church of St John, which wrought widespread damage in the surrounding area. From below the tower (east side), Theophiliskou Street, lined attractively with overhanging wooden balconies, stretches due east along the line of the **walls of the Byzantine city** which are visible at many points along its length: the regularly projecting **towers** (approximately every 25–30m) can also be discerned, often with mediaeval houses erected on top of them. In an area of excavation at the intersection of Theophiliskou and Panaitiou Streets, the talus of the ramparts can be seen; other sections are visible further down at the intersection with Lachitos Street, whose line passes through where the city gates would have stood.

Panaitiou Street returns north towards the Grand Master's Palace, heading into the heart of the area devastated by the explosion of the gunpowder cache which was ignited by a lightning strike in November 1856. Since there was, early on, a shortage of ammunition for the Knights during the siege of 1522, it remains a mystery why this cache was still here unused in the vaults of the Order's principal church. Nor was the quantity negligible: its explosion destroyed the church of St John, the bell-tower and observatory to the west, a large part of the Master's Palace and the buildings at the upper end of the Street of the Knights. What we see today in the area is restoration, although recent excavations have begun to reveal the foundations of the **church of St John** whose three-aisled nave lay in the area under where the neoclassical **Turkish School** building to the left now stands and whose transepts were where the street now runs. The church was founded in 1309/10 and was probably completed by 1325. It was of the severest simplicity as befitted a military church, and contained the sepulchres of the Masters of the Order of St John. Gustave Flaubert, who visited in 1850 shortly before its destruction, noted eight columns of porphyry inside—four to each side—surmounted with Corinthian-style capitals. After 1523 it was converted into a mosque. The Metropolitan Church of the Annunciation, constructed by the Italians in 1924/5 beside Mandraki harbour, is a close copy of its original form.

The church and the Grand Master's Palace were once joined by an arched portico or loggia. In 1937 a replica was built up by the Italians on the column-bases remaining from the destroyed 15th century structure. It now crowns the rise of the Street of the Knights.

The Grand Master's Palace

Like an orchestra of talented players brought together and forced unwillingly to perform a famous symphony, the **Grand Master's Palace** is an assemblage of many individual treasures and qualities, but a strangely indifferent whole. The crisp lines of its crenellations and round towers erected by the Italians between 1937 and 1940 are faithful to the general proportions and exterior appearance of what we know of the castle built by the Knights; but the interior has been substantially modified, the materials of the surfaces altered, and the spaces which saw so much important Mediaeval history are gone. Nonetheless the Palace contains many important treasures—**Ancient** and **Palaeochristian mosaics** set in the floors, antique furniture, two interesting **permanent exhibitions** on aspects of the history of Rhodes, as well as the ghost of a period of political aberration in recent Western history. All of this makes it a visit that should not be missed (*open June–Sept Tues–Sun 8–8, Mon 12.30–8; daily in winter, except Mon, 8.30–3. Entrance fee includes access to the exhibitions. Note: the two permanent exhibitions alternate days of opening – see below*).

HISTORY OF THE BUILDING

The Palace stands on a natural rise within the area of the ancient city on which the patronal Temple of Helios may once have stood: Lysippus's famous 'Quadriga (four-horse chariot) with the Sun' mentioned by Pliny (*Hist. Nat.*, XXXIV, 63), and—according to some proponents—the Colossus of Rhodes also may have stood here. The hill was used as an acropolis by the Byzantine city, which was of greatly reduced size by comparison with the ancient city. Some of the foundation walls of the Byzantine citadel were uncovered in the basement (north side) of the present building in 1988. The construction of a brand new, independent fortress of rectangular plan on the site was begun by the Knights not long after their arrival, probably in the period of Grand Master de Villeneuve (1319–46), and was completed by the end of the century. In peacetime it was the residence of the Master and the assembly place of the Order's councils; in war, it was designed so as to accommodate the citizenry and to resist a siege thanks to its strength and extensive, underground storage areas. Damaged and repaired in the period of the first siege (1480/1), it was little used by the Turkish victors after 1522 except as a prison. The building fell into decay, was damaged in an earthquake in 1851, and then reduced to its ruined ground-floor level by the accidental gunpowder explosion of 1856 in the vaults of the Church of St John just to its south.

The Italian Restoration

The monumental task of restoring the ruin was not a priority during the first 20 years of Italian occupation. But on the accession of Mussolini's close advisor, Cesare Maria de Vecchi, as Governor in 1936, the idea first appeared of making it into an appropriate residence for an eventual visit from either the *Duce* or the King of Italy. With unseemly haste and the extensive use of reinforced concrete clad in masonry, the building was re-erected between 1937 and 1940 under the supervision of Vittorio Mesturino, conforming in exterior appearance at least to the views and engravings which remained of the original palace; the interior was redesigned in a manner suitable for modern occupation and in a spirit appropriate to the political aspirations of Rome in the 1930s. Neither Mussolini nor Victor Emmanuel ever visited, and the work was not long completed when Italy was forced to relinquish the Dodecanese. On the right-hand side of the south entrance, opposite the ticket office, the two marble plaques commemorating the restoration in 1940—one written in Greek, the other in Italian—reveal in the language used the hidden aspirations and self-delusions of Fascist policy in Rhodes, as it sought constantly to sanction its actions through reference to the continuation of a glorious Roman/Latin tradition perpetuated through the Order of the Knights into modern times. The translated text is here cited in full:

In the reign of His Majesty Victor Emmanuel III,
King of Italy and of Albania, and Emperor of Ethiopia; un-
der Benito Mussolini, Duce of Fascism and Prime Minister:
Cesare Maria de Vecchi, Count of Val Cismon and
Governor of the Italian Islands of the Aegean,
restored and reconstructed this ancient castle—built over
unprofaned Roman ramparts by the Knights of St John,
Seat of Government, Stronghold of the Fortress, Defence
of Western Civilisation and of the Law and Religion of
Rome—giving Power and Splendour to its
Renewed History.
In the year of Our Lord, 1940—18th year of the Fascist Era.

Entrance, court & ground floor

The imposing **South Gate**—befitting a building that was primarily a fortress, and only secondarily a residence—flanked by two horse-shoe towers, communicates between the military parade court in front on the south side and the interior court of the castle. The chilling bareness of the central **courtyard** has little architectural relief: the insensitively 'finished' statues of Roman dignitaries on the opposite side, which were brought in 1937 from the ancient *Odeion* in Kos, are the sole figurative elements. In the original floor of the court were sunk a dozen large, circular grain stores; the marble 'well-heads' on the east side, marking three of them, were added by the Italians.

The lower floor of the north wing houses the well-displayed and clearly explained, permanent exhibition, '*Ancient Rhodes: 2400 Years*' (*open Wed, Fri and Sun*), covering the history of the city along thematic lines: Prehistoric beginnings and development (*Rooms 1 & 2*); public buildings and sanctuaries (*3*); the Rhodian house (*4*); domestic artefacts (*5*); cosmetics and daily life (*6*); artistic and spiritual life (*7*); ceramic workshops (*8*); work in bronze, glass, and terracotta (*9*); commerce and coinage (*10*); the cemetery (*11*); and burial customs (*12*). In the southwest corner is the second exhibition, '*Rhodes from the 4th century until the Turkish Conquest (1522)*' (*open Tues, Thur & Sat*) displays manuscripts and illustrated books, icons, finely decorated ceramics and objects of trade and ritual—together contributing a vivid sense of the colour of the city in the period. A pair of beautifully carved 16th century *wooden doors from the church of Aghia Triada, re-used (and perhaps partially restored) in Ottoman times, gives a valuable sense of the former appearance of the city's other many doorways, which today tend towards a drab uniformity.

On the wall to the left of the main interior stairs opposite the ticket office is a small **carved aedicule** with a 14th century sculptural group, in predominantly North Italian style, of the seated *Madonna and Child* (the latter, energetically holding up an Orb). Although it retains vestiges of original paint, the degree of erosion suggests that it was perhaps located on the exterior of a building. It somehow escaped destruction, and was immured here by the Italians in their restoration of the building. To the right of the staircase is the chapel of St Catherine (which once housed important relics of the saint), with a copy of Donatello's *St Nicholas of Bari*.

Upper floor State Rooms

In the **Hall** of the monumental staircase, the self-conscious patterning of the different colour-tones of the '*poros*' stone used in the facing of the walls by the Italian restorers is particularly noticeable. In the lowest area of the hall the original more serendipitous variegation of the Knights' masonry is visible, contrasting with the 'chess-board' artificiality of the 1930s work above.

The **State Rooms** of the *piano nobile* are spacious, high and luminous—not unpleasant, but indefinably lifeless because of their subjugation to an imposed idea of solemnity. Even the naturally joyous mosaics in the floors seem subdued. There are nearly two dozen ****panels of inlaid ancient mosaic**, taken from Late Hellenistic and Roman houses and from Early Christian basilicas on Kos, as well as from some buildings on Rhodes. Most came to light in Italian excavations in the wake of the 1933 earthquake on Kos. The '**Trophy' room** (*1: southwest corner*) exhibits one Hellenistic and one Early Christian mosaic, which never belonged together but show nonetheless the continuity of motif and method between the two epochs, separated by over 700 years. Their colours have been muted by the application of fixative and varnish. In the corner of the room is a 1st century BC **funerary trophy** from the southern necropolis of Rhodes on top of a finely decorated **Hellenistic altar** with scenes of Dionysos and dancing Maenads; the two pieces similarly never belonged together and relate awkwardly in both subject-matter and technical quality. In the adjacent room (*2*) is a cast of the famous *Laocoön* (now in the Vatican Collection in Rome), the most famous and representative work of Rhodian Hellenistic sculpture—solitary here, but once part of an ensemble of grand and dynamic pieces on Homeric themes, destined to be dramatically displayed in a grotto by the sea south of Rome.

The cross-vaulted room which projects under the tower in the middle of the west wing was the Governor's Office; in the adjacent **Audience Hall** (6) the Italian restorers' shaky grasp of architectural solutions is illustrated by the increasingly unhappy transition from column to capital. The splendid **5th century AD mosaic** on the floor comes from the Early Christian Basilica of Aghios Ioannis on Kos. The rooms also contain furniture of interest, including good **16th and 17th century wood-work** from Italian churches—candelabra, painted and gilded vestment-chests and, most notable of all, the two beautifully posed, **polychrome figures of the *Annunciation of the Virgin*** (late 15th century), in the **Room of the Nine Muses** (south wing, at end of itinerary). The room takes its name from a **floor-mosaic figuring the Muses** in a complex decorative design of linked roundels. A wide variety of styles and subjects is represented in the mosaics encountered in the circuit of the rooms: decorative 'tapestries' of birds, fishes and plants; finely detailed *emblemata* (centrepiece medallions) such as that of *Medusa* (*4*) and a *Nymph riding a sea-horse* (*8*); and mythological narratives such as the scene of *Poseidon defeating Polybotes* (corridor of east wing)—of particular local interest because of its connection with the story of the origin of the island of Nisyros.

A different external view of the Palace as a whole, and its well-articulated mass as seen from the north, can be obtained from the walk through the moat of the walls (entered from Plateia Alexandrias by the taxi stand). In the north-facing stretch of wall before the Tower of Plaignes is the only remaining carved emblem with the three *fasces* of the Fascist period. Nearby is also an Ottoman commemorative plaque in Osmanli script.

The Street of the Knights

From the arched loggia before the outer entrance to the Grand Master's Palace, Ippotón Street, the '**Street of the Knights**', leads steeply down to the east following the line of one of the main arterial, east/west streets of the Hippodamian plan of the Ancient city.

Photographs from the beginning of the last century show the street overhung by wooden, Ottoman balconies and *sachnisia*, and with a vibrant street-life which contrasts markedly with today's rather museified air. Even so, when Flaubert visited Rhodes in 1850 he commented on the 'silence' of the street: '*le ton… est plus triste que beau*'. The street has seen much damage—acts of war (modern and mediaeval), earth-quakes, accidental explosions, and ideological renovations in which the buildings were purged of their Turkish accre-tions and substantially reconstructed by the Italians in the 1930s. Throughout all this, it has still retained its original di-mensions and the colour of its stone, and remains one of the completest and most homogeneous Mediaeval streets in the Eastern Mediterranean. It stretches symbolically between the two most important poles of the Order of the Knights of St John: the complex of the cathedral of St John and the Grand Master's Palace, with all that they symbolise of the higher spiritual ideals of the Order and the rigorous discipline of its organisation, at the top of the street; and the Hospital at the bottom of the hill, representing the Order's commit-ment to the worldly sufferings of the sick and poor. In be-tween, stretch the national representations and conventual residences of the Knights—the noblest, secular buildings of the city, whose beauty and tranquility lie in a number of important aesthetic contrasts: between the honey-coloured stone and the dense vegetation enclosed, between the dark vaulted spaces and the wells of light they surround, and be-tween the *chochlakia* pavements, decorated balustrades and ornate window-frames and the plain masonry of the walls which they embellish. The lower floor of these buildings is normally a service courtyard surrounded by vaulted storage areas and stables, from which broad, open steps lead up to the high-ceilinged living and reception rooms on the upper floor.

The oldest and best-preserved of these conventual buildings is the **Inn of the Tongue of Spain** near the top of the street on the south side. The interior can be visited (entrances both from Ippotón and Ippárchou Streets). The main entrance is distinguished by the Aragonese design of its arch with characteristically wide voussoirs—longer even than the radius of the open arch they form. This is one of the few façades in which elements have survived from before the siege of 1480; the original, mid-15th century masonry on the ground floor differs noticeably from that above. Steps lead up to the large **hall** on the first floor, which though re-roofed and restored, still preserves its airy proportions and some of the original patterned floor. Opposite is the **Inn of the Tongue of Provence** (1518), with a decorated portal surmounted by four coats of arms set in a cross-shaped niche. A little downhill to the east, a plethora of panels with carved escutcheons in various combinations (among them the arms of England appear repeatedly) mark the residence of the '**Prior of the Church**' (now the Italian Consulate) and the adjacent domed chapel of the **Holy Trinity**. The unusual central plan of the tiny church suggests that the Knights may have adapted a pre-existing Byzantine church on this site to their own use, during the time of Grand Master Raymond Bérenger (1365–65). The **sculpture of the Madonna and Child** beneath a canopy on the corner—the only figurative relief in the street—is of the same period, and has remarkably survived in the position for which it was originally intended.

Lower down, the north side of the street is dominated by the imposing front of the **Inn of the Tongue of France**, distinguished by its four rounded turrets and projecting water-spouts elaborately carved as dragons' mouths, recalling the exploits of Dieudonné de Gozon with the Dragon of Malpasso (*see p. 158*). The **window cornices** are soberly decorated and the horizontality of the façade is enhanced by carved **string-courses**, whose calibrated steps allow them to follow the gentle slope of the street. The whole is a pleasing synthesis of Gothic elements combined into a façade organised according to new Renaissance principles. Although a preceding French 'Auberge' stood here before the siege of 1480, the present building was begun in 1492 (hence the arms of Pierre d'Aubusson) and finished around 1512 (arms of Emery d'Amboise). The building was purchased in 1912 by the French Ambassador to the Ottoman court, Maurice Bompard, and was later restored by the French historian, architect and specialist in both Ottoman and Mediaeval art, Albert Gabriel in 1939.

The west end of the Inn of France is bounded by a small alleyway that leads north to the **House of Djem** (left side) entered through a white marble door-frame (1512), carved with acanthus capitals and small rosettes which relieve the classicising purity of its Renaissance design. The house takes its name from the Ottoman prince who was lodged here during the summer of 1482.

CEM, SON OF THE CONQUEROR

In the austere world of the Order of St John the exotic figure of the Turkish prince, Cem, sounds a note of colourful relief. In 1481, the year after the first siege of Rhodes, Mehmet II, conqueror of Byzantium, died and his succession was bitterly contested between his two sons, Cem (whose name, a contraction of 'Jemshid', is pronounced '*jem*' and generally written 'Djem' or 'Zizim' in the west) and his more introverted elder brother, who went on to rule as Beyazit II. Thwarted in his bid for power, Cem turned to the Knights of St John and negotiated a potentially risky political asylum in their hands, at

first promising perpetual peace between the Ottoman Empire and Christendom if the Knights helped
him overthrow his brother. He had had contact with
the Knights before when he was Governor of Konya
and the Southwest Provinces under his father. Grand
Master d'Aubusson welcomed the possibility since
the prince's presence on the island, if handled cor-
rectly, could guarantee some measure of peace with
the Turks. The prince was transferred to a Hospitaller
galley at sea and later received in the city with great
ceremony in July of 1482. The Master escorted him
personally to his specially prepared lodgings beside
the Inn of France. Illustrations from the contemporaneous Caoursin Codex show the prince being en-
tertained to dinner by the Grand Master. When em-
issaries from Istanbul arrived to sue for the prince's
return, Cem was moved to France for greater safety
in September of the same year. d'Aubusson exploited
the situation adeptly, securing a yearly allowance of
45,000 ducats to keep the prince under permanent
guard eventually in the castle of Bourganeuf in the
Auvergne. In addition, Beyazit sent the Order one
of Constantinople's most precious relics—the right

arm of St John the Baptist which had been kept in the capital since the 10th century. The prince's lengthy journey from Nice to Bourganeuf was punctuated with amorous intrigues in the aristocratic houses that offered hospitality along the way—at Roussillon, Puy and at Sassenage, where his host's daughter, Hélène, became the object of his affections. In 1484 the circular, fortified 'Tower of Zizim' was completed at Bourganeuf to house the prince and his retinue: each day he bathed, versified, and drank spiced wine in spite of Koranic proscriptions. His poems are beautifully rendered in English by Elias Gibb, in his collection *Ottoman Poems*, published in London in 1882. He was too valuable a hostage however to survive for long: Pope Innocent VIII demanded his presence in Rome for a planned crusade in 1489. His successor, Alexander VI Borgia, imprisoned him. Charles VIII of France took him back from the Pope in 1494. And the following year Cem died at the age of 35 in Capua, north of Naples—supposedly poisoned, and still in the custody of Charles. He was later buried in Bursa.

Further north (now inaccessible), the Gothic church of St Demetrius (1499) overlies remains of an ancient temple, possibly of Dionysos, which was famed in Antiquity for its works of art. Beyond have been found remains of ancient ship-sheds underneath the later (2nd century AD) base of a Roman, monumental tetrapylon at the crossing of two ancient streets.

In Láchitos Street, off the south side of Ippoton Street. (across from the House of Djem), is the **House of Admiral Costanzo Operti** (right), one of the few surviving examples of a bourgeois, civil residence dating from the period of the Knights. The core of the house—the design of the façade and of the principal window-frames—dates from 1517; but there have been numerous additions and modifications over time. (*The building is currently under restoration.*)

Opposite the Inn of France is the **Mansion of Diomed de Villaragut**, built around a courtyard of cypress trees with an inscribed 19th century Ottoman fountain at its centre. The central gate is surmounted, as in the Inn of Spain, by an arch with wide voussoirs in the Aragonese manner—giving it a feel of importance and impregnability. Villaragut was Victualler to the Grand Master and Captain of the Tongue of Aragon from 1497 to 1504. The building suffered war damage in the last century. Its eastern wing has currently been adapted to host the *Prehis-*

toric Collection of the Archaeological Museum, to which it is adjacent.

The two buildings which flank the lower end of the Street of the Knights are the **Inn of the Tongue of Italy** (much restored) of 1519 (north side—now the offices of the Archaeological Department) and the Hospital of the Knights, whose subsidiary entrance on the south side of this street is framed with a portal of unexpected grandeur in the finest Gothic style.

The Hospital of the Knights and the Rhodes Archaeological Museum

The building

This was the Knights' second, or 'Great Hospital', built 80 years after its mid-14th century predecessor on the west side of Argyrokastrou Square. The carved inscription above the main entrance refers to the founding of a new '*Xenodocheio*' (travellers' lodgings) by Grand Master Antonio Fluviã (1421–37) who endowed it with a gift of 10,000 Florins in his will. Construction was only begun in July 1440 under his successor, Jean de Lastic. It was badly damaged in the siege of 1480 and was only finally in service towards the end of the same decade. Although tending to the sick was a primary mission of the Knights, their title of 'Hospitallers' also referred to the hospitality and protection they were obliged to give to pilgrims travelling to and from the Holy Land. Only a part of this building, therefore, functioned as a hospital for the sick, the rest being given over to lodgings for pilgrims and their horses—hence the appearance it has externally and internally of a *caravanserai*, with stables and storage spaces below and sleeping quarters above. The building is conceived with customary military simplicity. The long plain façade above the row of arched magazine entrances is relieved only by two string-courses and the apse-like projection above the **main gate**, whose simple and dignified decoration and vertical mouldings are more appreciable by contrast. The original cypress-wood doors, divided into 34 panels intricately carved with decorative designs and archangels, were given by Sultan Mahmud II in 1836 to Louis-Philippe of France and are now in Versailles. The relief above the gate shows angels holding the Fluviā arms beneath the banner of the Order with the dedicatory inscription below. The proceeds from renting out as shops the row of seven independent 'magazines' to either side of the entrance helped defray the expenses of the hospital and its work. The **interior courtyard**—substantially restored by Amedeo Mauri between 1913 and 1918, and again in 1949 after war damage—has an even greater, monastic chastity to it. The surfaces are unadorned except for some minimal attention to the capitals from which the ribs and vaults spring.

This starkness is in contrast to the effect of the beautiful **Infirmary Ward* which occupies the entire length of the east side on the upper level and is one of the finest interior spaces in Rhodes. The diffused natural light, airy spaciousness and noble proportions of this long rectangular hall, with its elegant procession of high, Gothic arches down the centre, must have exerted a benign influence on the sufferings of those confined here. The space must be imagined furnished with its 32 beds canopied with fine brocade—the tranquility disturbed only by the hushed movements of the nurses and surgeons who were permanently on duty and the sputtering of the fire-place at the south end of the room. Its similarity to the 'Hall of the Poor' in Chancellor Rolin's *Hôtel-Dieu* in Beaune, founded in the same years, is striking. The focus of the room was the **exedra** in the centre of the east wall, framed by a wide arch decorated with flamboyant tracery; here, below the high windows, stood the altar where mass was celebrated daily. To both sides, small doorways lead into windowless cubicles which probably served to provide a measure of privacy for the more intimate operations and examinations which the treatment of the patients on occasions required. It should be recalled that men and women patients were not segregated.

THE TREATMENT OF PATIENTS

The Hospitaller of the Order was by tradition the head of the *Langue de France*. He appointed, for a period of two years, one of the Knights as the 'Infirmarer', whose job it was to supervise the doctors, surgeons, apothecaries and nurses of the Infirmary. Patients did not pay for treatment, but they were obliged to abide by the rules of the hospital which hung on a chain in the main hall. These enforced tranquility and quiet, and obliged every patient to be confessed on admission and to draw up a will, to abstain from gambling and to read only material of a religious nature. As elsewhere in the Mediaeval world, physicians (superior in status) and surgeons (considered more as artesans) worked independently. When amputation was necessary, the hospital would provide a certificate attesting that the intervention was as the result of injury and not a punishment for crimes. Patients were allowed a personal servant; they were allotted an individual bed and cubicle, and ate from silver plate for what were considered reasons of hygiene. They were visited twice daily by the physicians on duty, as well as by the Infirmarer in person.

A number of the Grand Masters' funerary monuments and escutcheons salvaged from the church of St John after its destruction have been collected together here: at the north end, the **arms of Juan Fernandez de Heredia** (1377–96) with bronze lettering and dark stone inlay for the coat of arms, and an Antique sarcophagus reworked as the tomb of Pierre de Corneillan (1353–55); at the southeast corner, the finely carved royal arms of England (c. 1400) in grey, Lardos marble. The coats of arms (originally coloured) around the capitals of the seven central pillars are those of the Order and of the Grand Master Pierre d'Aubusson (1476–1503) under whom the building was completed and who himself was successfully healed of seemingly fatal wounds received during the siege of 1480 by the surgeons and doctors of the Hospital. To the south, the Infirmary communicates with a series of rooms which included a pharmacy, refectory, kitchens and other service areas. These contain elements of the Archaeological Collection, which for many is the main reason for visiting this building.

The Archaeological Collection

(*Open daily, except Mon, June–Sept 8–7; Oct–May 8–3.*)

This is an important, though uneven, archaeological collection—long on grave-goods, pottery and votive offerings, but short on the great sculpture of the Rhodian School which was of such renown in later Antiquity. One of the finest exhibits of the museum, however, can be visited before entering the building—in the northernmost magazine on the ground floor of the exterior façade, on the corner of the Street of the Knights: it is a display of thirteen magnificent 7th and 6th century BC, *funerary jars or *pithoi*, standing between 150 and 180cm in height and mostly decorated with moulded, abstract designs and elaborately fenestrated handles. They come from the Archaic cemetery at Kameiros. Notwithstanding their impressive size, these were generally (though not always) used for the burial of infants and children—as though the burial of the tiny folded body, with feet at the bottom and head towards the entrance, was a return in death to the security of the maternal womb. Adults by contrast were mostly cremated in this period. Although the *pithos* was generally a household storage vessel, these ones distinguish themselves as ritual burial-receptacles by their attention to overall decoration. One of them, at the end of the room, bears a circle of small drill holes, perhaps for the application of a thin metal plaque or medallion; another, to the right, though plain bears the name 'ERGIAS' on the rim. Two ancient granary pits are visible sunk below the floor of the room.

Ground floor—courtyard

Facing the entrance across the courtyard is a **recumbent lion** with the head of a bull held between its paws, carved from local Rhodian marble. It is a grave-marker of the Hellenistic period, with the unmistakable symbolism appropriate to a high-ranking military official. In front of it is a small area of the **mosaic floor** from the 5th century, Early Christian basilica of Eucharistos at Arkása on the east coast of Karpathos; another *larger mosaic of remarkable decorative beauty, with a vine border and motifs of fish and bird, from the 6th century Basilica of Aghia Anastasia also at Arkása, is displayed in the inner courtyard to the south. Though dusty today, these mosaics should be imagined with their naturally brilliant colours polished by the constant abrasion of feet and illuminated by the candlelight of the basilicas. Around the perimeter of both the courtyard and the upper gallery, decorated altars, *stelai*, inscribed pedestals and other epigraphic fragments are exhibited.

Upper floor—sculpture rooms

(The five rooms of the Sculpture Collection are in the south-east corner of the upper floor, with access from a passage at the south end of the main Infirmary ward.)

Notable in the first hall (*Room II*), formerly the Hospital Refectory, are the 3rd century AD, **grave stelai from Nisyros** with naïvely carved figures of the deceased seen frontally, with one arm folded across the breast—a pose reminiscent of their Cycladic forebears of three millennia earlier. Three reliefs of a mounted Oriental deity with a club are testimony to the arrival of new eastern cults into the late Roman Empire. *Room III* contains the collection's few exhibits from the Archaic and Classical periods, dominated by the well-conserved and justly famous ***grave stele of Krito** taking leave of her mother, Tamarista (c. 420 BC). This is the work of a period in which the dignified flow and counter-flow of the draperies are still actively felt by the artist and have not yet become mere, rhetorical pattern: a comparison with the mid-4th century BC stele of Kalliarista (to left, in the same room) illustrates this. The partial fore-shortening of Krito's left leg and foot is also noteworthy. The room contains some fine 6th century BC, Archaic pieces from neighbouring islands, and two Cycladic marble *kouroi* from Kameiros probably produced in the workshops of Paros or Naxos. There is also a rare, **7th century** BC **perirrhanterion** (a water-stoup for ritual purification) incorporating in its complex design the repeated image of a female divinity standing on a crouching lion, whose tail she holds in one hand and a leash in the other.

Rooms IV, V & VI contain sculpture from the time of the founding of the city of Rhodes (408/7 BC) to the Hellenistic and Roman Age—a period in which the sturdy volumes and strong tactile appeal of earlier sculpture were replaced by fine 'draughtsmanship' and elegant cutting. There is a new accent on movement, on drapery as an expression of that movement, and on the narrative aspect of a piece. The pretty **Crouching Aphrodite**—a 1st century BC copy in small scale of an original by the 3rd century sculptor Doidalsas of Bythinia (an artist of whom little is known for certain but who probably worked in the circle of Lysippus)—is an example of this new decorative trend. This is not contemplative or sacred art, but rather the centre-piece of a fountain or pool of water in which the attractive pose was mirrored. The mid 2nd century BC ***Aphrodite Pudica**, related in design to Praxiteles's famous Aphrodite of Cnidus was, on the other hand, a cult statue perhaps from the Temple of Aphrodite by the Commercial Harbour. Immortalised by Lawrence

Durrell as the 'Marine Venus', she was recovered from the sea north of the harbour of Rhodes. The definition of her features have an impressionistic soft-focus: this is the result of erosion by sea-water which has imparted to the marble a translucence akin to the original effect of *ganosis*—the waxing and polishing of marble statuary practised by the Ancient Greeks. Of the same period and school, are the two studies of a **Nymph on a Rock**, in different poses, differing styles and a variety of different finishes to the marble. The rooms also exhibit some notable portraits and heads: a 3rd century BC **head of Dionysos** wearing a vine wreath, in *rosso antico* (not porphyry as labelled); a 2nd century BC **head of Helios** with perforations for the affixing of golden sun-rays to the crown of the head, whose pose is based on the Lysippan 'portraits' of Alexander the Great; and from the Roman period, an interesting **portrait of Antoninus Pius**, and a copy of a popular 3rd century BC portrait of the dramatist Menander. The cheeks and the eyes of the latter have the remarkable sensitivity of a painter's shadows.

Room II leads out onto the terrace of the courtyard garden where there is a collection of funerary monuments, sculptures and decorative Hellenistic pieces, such as the fine, sporting dolphin. In the future this area will communicate directly with the Prehistoric and Epigraphic collections to be housed in a wing of the adjacent Vil-laragut Mansion.

Upper floor—funerary and votive deposits, pottery and small objects

Both of the Ancient cities of Ialysos and Kameiros and their surrounding settlements have yielded an extraordinary wealth of material from their cemeteries and from the votive deposits of their respective sanctuaries of Athena. This is displayed in the 15 small rooms which form the south, west and north sides of the upper courtyard. The international provenance of some of the material and designs shows that Rhodes early on had trading and cultural links with a wide area of the lands surrounding the Mediterranean and the Black Sea. The first three rooms (*south side*) display 8th and 9th century BC grave finds from the area of Ialysos and modern Kremastí; these are pieces with only **Geometric designs** of crystalline clarity, except for a few 8th century BC *oenochoai* with anthropomorphic spouts in the form of heads. A case with 6th century BC items in grey-ware from graves at Tsambikos includes a vase (*no. 9*) of beautiful form with an unusual, 'faux-marble' type of decoration. The first two rooms of the *west side* have 6th century BC black-figure ware: amongst them an exquisite *circular pyxis (a small, lidded storage-vase), with clear and beautiful abstract designs to either side of a procession of Chukar partridges, depicted in varying poses around the shoulder of the piece. In the third room, amongst the mostly red-figure ware from graves, is a 5th century BC, **painted marble discus** with the figure of a discus-thrower, probably from an athlete's grave.

With the long *rectangular room* on the west side begins the collection of **votive offerings from the sanctuaries of Athena**, first at Ialysos. This is an extraordinary variety and display of small objects, stretching from the 8th century to the 4th century BC, often showing oriental influence in design and material: this is the first we see of objects in ivory, precious stones, bronze, glass, and glass-paste. A case with early 6th century BC **figurines in limestone from Cyprus** includes several examples of the '*moscophoros*' image—a young offrand bearing a sacrificial animal, holding it with arms crossed over the chest. Offerings found at the sanctuary of Athena at Kameiros, again including Egyptian and Cypriot artefacts, continue in the northwest corner of the *north side*. The next four rooms along the north side are devoted to finds from the cemeteries at Kameiros—including many of the gifts which accompanied the infant burials in the large decorated *pithoi* which are exhibited in the ground-floor vault of the museum (*see above*). These include stemmed cups and dishes of the Geometric period—at first with clear, abstract designs, then later with zoomorphic designs, such as a running hare or the small terracotta figure of a donkey carrying vessels. Other domestic items include: a painted knee-guard used in wool-working; a delicate bronze mirror; an extraordinarily well-preserved, early 5th century BC, painted **Attic vessel in the shape of a female head**, signed by the potter—'Midas made me' (*no. 30*). The collection concludes with two rooms of selected 8th to 5th century BC **Rhodian**, **Corinthian** and **Attic pottery** of great sophistication—many of the pieces decorated with captivating depictions of birds and running animals—and a display of bronze and glass artefacts from the graves at Kameiros.

The entrance to the Knights Hospital faces the narrow opening of the **Arnaldo Gate**, due east across the attractive Museum Square. The entrance to the gate on the inside is flanked by two buildings: to the south is the **Inn of the Tongue of England**, originally erected in 1482, almost destroyed during the 19th century, and rebuilt on the original plan by Col. Sir Vivian Gabriel and repaired by the British in 1949. The north wall bears a large panel of restored coats of arms of England (only the left hand corner is original), set in an extravagant **ogival frame** with

oak-leaf motif. Opposite to the north is the open portico
of the House of Guy de Melay, similarly restored 'in style'
by Armando Bernabiti in 1930.

The church of St Mary of the Castle

Facing up the length of the Street of the Knights from its
lower end is the grand **church of St Mary of the Castle**, or
of the **Panaghia tou Kastrou** (*open daily, except Mon, 8.30–
3*). The façade is militarily bare in design, although its central, corniced panel was probably decorated in the 15th
century with a mural of the Virgin Mary as Protectress of
the Castle, flanked by Saints and Knights of the Order.

The building

The church was first raised in the 11th century as the **Panaghia tou Kastrou**, the Greek Orthodox Cathedral of Rhodes,
on an inscribed cross-in-square floor-plan—a design not
particularly common on Rhodes. Within the first decade of
the Knights' arrival in 1309, its damaged and probably un-
finished structure was almost entirely rebuilt as the Roman
Catholic Cathedral of St Mary, referred to in a Papal Bull
of Pope John XXII of 1322. The interior was transformed
and the barrel-vaults of the aisles and crossings given Gothic
elegance and verticality by the ribs of cross-vaults and the
inclusion of a clerestory of pointed windows. The interior is

luminous and airy: originally there was stained glass—visible as late as 1826 when it was drawn by the Belgian artist, Witdoeck—which modified its light. After 1522, a minaret, *mihrab* and porch with three cupolas (west front) were added and the building was used for Islamic worship as the 'Enderum Cami'.

Paintings

Inside the mostly unadorned interior of the church are areas of paintings of two kinds: those decorating the church itself, and those brought here for safety from elsewhere.

In the first group are patches of 13th century, Byzantine wall-paintings of saints and martyrs, which have been retrieved from under the Turkish whitewash on the pillars of the eastern arch. In a markedly different, Western style, is the late 14th century **figure of St Lucy** on the west wall, which dates from the Hospitaller period. The pale fresco tints and the modelling of her eyes and brows are probably the work of a North Italian artist, close to the circle of Altichiero.

The second kind of paintings displayed here are the detached wall-paintings which are of two separate origins: the first, to the north side are **Byzantine wall-paintings from the monastery of St Michael at Tharri**. These include two late 12th century figures of Church Fathers, and a series of early 17th century paintings from the drum and dome of the *catholicon*, which are grand in scale and clear in style. These were removed in 1972 during restoration to the building so as to reveal layers of earlier painting *in situ* beneath. The second group, in the southeast corner, are late 14th century paintings salvaged in 1984 from the tiny, dilapidated church of Aghios Zacharias on the island of Chalki (*see p. 258*). These are in poor condition, but a dramatic *Christ Harrowing Hell*, in which the Saviour wrests Adam from Limbo, is of considerable stylistic quality.

The courtyard

An area to the north side of the church exhibits a collection of fragments and marble elements from carved, Byzantine templon screens. Sections of mosaic floor are also displayed: the fine 'cosmatesque' **panel of inlaid polychrome marbles** in the centre, comes from the excavation of the Early Christian basilica on Heimáras and P. Melá Sreets in the west of the city (*see p. 147*).

Around Argyrokastrou Square

To the north of the church of St Mary of the Castle, the street passes underneath an arch into Argyrokastrou Square with the 16th century **Inn of the Tongue of Auvergne** to the right. The building was heavily restored in 1919, although the fine portal on the south façade is mostly original and bears an inscription with the date 1507. Through the arch and to the left, the western side of the cobbled square is bounded by a pleasing assemblage of buildings which comprised the First Hospital of the Knights, built under Grand Master Roger de Pins (arms on façade) between 1355 and 1365—one of the few buildings to survive intact from before the siege of 1480. The building is often referred to as the 'Armoury', since it was used as such by the Turks and probably also by the Knights after the commissioning of the new hospital building. Its most beautiful element is the main **entrance façade** which, although it has lost elements of its projecting stone porch, has a fine arched portal flanked by elegant lancet windows and surmounted by a moulded string-course and crenellations. It was formerly the apse of the hospital chapel, and its present appearance is the result of modifications carried out under Fabrizio del Carretto at the beginning of the 16th century. In the reconstructed (1920) arcade to its south is the entrance to the **Historical Institute and Library of the Dodecanese**. In the centre of the square is a fountain composed of Byzantine marble elements, most of which constituted a 6th century baptismal font, decorated with crosses, which was found near the village of Arnítha in the south of the island. It is surrounded by sizeable stone balls from the 1522 siege. The south wing of the building is occupied by the delightful *Museum of Decorative Arts of the Dodecanese which contains little that is not of first-class quality (*open daily, except Mon, 8.30–3*). The objects displayed come from a wide variety of the islands and are exhibited not in rigid classifications but in decorative arrangements loosely inspired by the interiors which they once adorned.

Three categories in particular are well represented: ceramics, wooden furniture and embroidered textiles. There is an ample collection of Turkish *Iznik ceramics, ranging from early 16th century pieces in blue and green only, to the beautiful variety of colours used in the 17th century for tableware, tankards and decorative elements for the interior of mosques. This is complemented by the more earthy colours and figurative folk-motifs of ceramics from Kütahya and Çanakkale. The pieces are exhibited together with later (Rhodian) 'Lindos ware' which maintained the motifs and designs of Iznik ceramic into the 18th century. Much of the woodwork is finely carved and painted: the 18th century doors and **bed-heads from Patmos**, and an early 19th century **carved *moussandra*** (a large, raised platform used as a bed and storage space) from Symi, stand out. The embroidery of the textiles has the tender colours (especially reds and pale-greens) associated with vegetable dyes; the examples exhibited are not purely ceremonial items, but such everyday necessities as towels and sheets which were nonetheless of exquisite manufacture. By the entrance door is the front of a wooden chest painted with what appears to be an inebriated recollection of the Piazzetta of San Marco in Venice.

The continuation of the Armoury buildings to the north houses the (Old) **Municipal Art Gallery** (*open daily, except Sun, 8–2*).

Since the opening of the New Rhodes Art Gallery in G. Haritos Square in the New Town (*see p. 129*) this space is dedicated to rotating displays of works by local Rhodian artists. It also contains the Noel Rees Collection of **prints and maps** of Rhodes and the Dodecanese which provides an interesting picture of Rhodes and the Islands before the 20th century. Commander Noel Rees (who died in 1947) was a Hellenophile and Consul in Smyrna, who served the cause of Greek nationalism by helping many (amongst them several notable politicians) escape from occupied Greece through a network of secret routes through the Aegean. He was half-Greek on the side of his mother whose family was from Chios.

The Temple of Aphrodite and Symis Square

To the east, in the open area in front of the building, are the remains of the 3rd century BC **Temple of Aphrodite**, uncovered by Italian archaeologists in 1922. The temple—as was customary with shrines to Aphrodite who was a patron divinity of sailors—occupied a prime location between the commercial and military ports.

It was perhaps the lack of space in this crowded area of Ancient Rhodes which gave rise to the unusual form of the temple—pro-style *in antis*, with a colonnade of half-engaged columns on the longer sides, designed so as not to take up any more space than necessary. The poor quality of the stone used meant that it would originally have been dressed with stucco. The fact that different elements from the temple and the surrounding area have been stored and erected on top of the foundations without respect to the building's original design, does not permit a clear reading of the site. The building was oriented east–west; the long sides had the engaged colonnade, and the two column stumps now placed along their length, may originally have served to support the east portico. Much of the heavily decorated entablature, now lying in sections on the ground along the north side, is Roman work and dates from restoration carried out in the 3rd century AD, under Diocletian. It is possibly from this temple that the statue of Aphrodite '*Pudica*' (Durrell's 'Marine Venus') now in the Archaeology Museum, came.

To the south of the temple excavations are currently continuing: these extend into the area in front of the early 19th century, Ottoman residence which closes Argyrokastrou Square to the east, known as the '**mansion of Hassan Bey**'—with its characteristic stone-carved lattice windows for ventilation in the attic of the building.

To the north of the temple is the large open space of **Symis Square**, bounded to north and east by the city walls. At this point, they are built over the ancient, **Hellenistic walls and fortifications**, which are clearly visible at a lower level between the St Paul and Liberty Gates. Above, at ground level, in the corner is an **armaments store** bearing the (still coloured) arms of Grand Master Jacques de Milly (1454–61). The vaulted interior is unrelieved except for the low slits for essential ventilation. Opposite is a small, decorative Ottoman fountain.

Of the three gates in this area; the main '**Liberty Gate**' is a modern breach in the walls created for motorised traffic by the Italians in 1924. To its east is the **Gate of St Paul**, erected in the mid 15th century under Jacques de Milly, which was the main communication between the two harbours. To the south, and giving onto the Commercial Harbour is the **Arsenal** ('**Tarsana**') **Gate**, whose broad, low form was originally designed to permit boats to slip from a boatyard in this area into the water. It was sealed up before the 1480 siege, and only opened again under Turkish dominion.

CENTRAL SECTOR: SOUTH OF SOKRATOUS STREET & THE MARINE GATE, AND WEST OF PYTHAGORA STREET

This area of the mediaeval city is a labyrinth of tiny, crooked streets, on which it is hard to impose a foolproof and logical itinerary for visiting its many monuments. Two itineraries in the form of loops are outlined below: the first (eastern) loop, beginning at the Marine Gate on the Main Harbour, covers what is seen in the area of the rectangle of Pythagóra, Omírou, and Aghiou Phanaríou Streets, finishing at the Mehmet Agha Mosque on Sokrátous Street; the second (western) loop begins at the Mehmet Agha Mosque, winds through Ariónos Square to the St Athanasius Gate, and returns down Ippodámou and Sokrátous Streets to where it began.

The Marine Gate

The **Marine Gate** was the front door of the city through which all outside visitors first passed, having disembarked in the Commercial Harbour. It breaks the faceless curtain of the harbour walls: its massive volumes—no less impressive than those of the d'Amboise Gate—are here taller and more eloquent of importance than practical for defence. There is a double door-frame in marble inside, with two guard rooms on either side in the passage. Above the gate are the eroded statues of the Virgin Mary (Protectress of the City), St John (Protector of the Knights' Order) and (?) St Peter, whose presence here may refer to the fact that it was receipts from Rome in the Jubilee Year announced by Sixtus IV for 1477 that funded the construction of the gate's two towers, erected by Grand Master Pierre d'Aubusson in the following year.

The Marine Gate leads immediately into the liveliest area of the town. One block directly ahead of the gate (west, up Aeólou Street) is an area of open excavation where the foundations of the eastern wall of the **Byzantine fortifications** of the city can be seen below the ruins of a Turkish *hamam*. The *hamam* was part of the complex of the 19th century **Shadirvan Mosque** (10m to south on Aristoménous Street), whose bold octagonal form and imposing height dominate the surrounding skyline.

The main street however leads directly to the left into **Ip-pokrátous Square**, the heart of the Greek commercial area of the Old Town. The arcaded fronts of the shops which border the square were created in an overall redesigning of the space by the Italian architect Florestano di Fausto in 1929/30; shortly after that date, the fountain in 'Italianate Mediaeval' style was added.

The Castellanía

The building which dominates the square to the east is the ***Castellanía** whose principal floor, built over an open loggia below, is approached by a flight of external steps rising to a terrace offering a good panorama over the lower part of the city. The building housed the city's Penal and Commercial Courts in the time of the Knights. Under the Turks the upper floor became a Prayer Hall (the 'Bedesten Cami') and the lower portico, a fish-market: today it is home, more appropriately, to the city's Municipal Library and Archives which look onto the courtyard garden behind the building.

Built in 1507, it bears (west front) the arms of Grand Master Emery d'Amboise in white marble supported by two *hommes sauvages* and set in a highly **ornate Gothic frame**. The window below has fine white, decorated marble mullions. The *sculpted doorframe** at the top of the steps is the building's most unusual and beautiful decoration: its slightly awkward setting, pressed into the corner, suggests that it might have been moved from another site. Within a highly classicising border of bound bay-leaves, an archangel holds the arms of the Order and of Emery d'Amboise against a field of flame-bursts which fills the door-frame like the background of a tapestry. To both sides stylised trees (with something of the appearance of artichokes) support two further coats of arms, that of the Knight, Ignacio de Ayala (left), and of Philippe Villiers de l'Isle Adam ('Grand Hospitaller' at the time, and later Grand Master of the Order). The south façade is pleasingly articulated with ornately moulded window-frames, overhung by a row of grotesque, zoomorphic water-spouts above. In the interior the wooden ceilings are decorated with surviving, early 16th century paintings and decorative motifs.

To the west of the square rises Sokrátous Street, the main commercial thoroughfare of the Old Town today and of the Ottoman, Mediaeval, Byzantine and Ancient cities before. To the south is Pythagóra St, following the line of one of the arteries of Ancient Rhodes's Hippodamian grid-plan. The first loop begins by following the latter.

The Mosque of Ibrahim Pasha

The second street to the west from Pythagóra Street leads into the plane-shaded square in front of the **Ibrahim Pasha Cami** founded in 1531, which today is the principal, functioning mosque of the city's Moslem community and for that reason has been substantially restored, first in 1928 by the Italians (who re-erected the minaret on its original base) and again in the last ten years. A domed, square prayer-hall with richly decorated wood-work is preceded by a wide, raised porch. To the west, beyond the mosque's canopied fountain, is an open area (Plátonos Street) with excavations at considerable depth below ground level.

At the lower level, below later overbuilding, is visible the base of Byzantine walls to the right (running north/south); and to the north side are the 4th century BC walls that bordered the ancient port, which at that time penetrated deeper inland. At an acute angle to it, is the base of another structure with a protruding, square aedicule (?tower), entered from the south west side, which overlooked the ancient harbour.

Pythagóra Street

As Pythagóra Street rises to the south it passes underneath the *****Hadji Halil Mansion**, built between 1880–90 in an elegant, neoclassical style. The tower of the abandoned house which straddles the street, with its pedimented façade of triple, round-arched windows, is a landmark in the city. The framed entrance-door (east side of street) leads into a couple of courtyards paved in pebbles with attractive sunburst and cypress-tree designs (dated 1903): a gently curving external wooden staircase leads to the main, upper floor of the building. To the east of the building lies an acre of citrus fruit-orchard which is entirely walled, traversed by water channels and irrigation cisterns and thronging with bird-life. With gardens to both sides of the street, this was one of the Old Town's most gracious dwellings in the last years of Ottoman occupation.

Pythagóra Street runs just to the east of the line of the outer **Byzantine walls** of the city. These emerge into view just beyond the Hadji Halil Mansion in the excavated area of Konti Square. Bisecting the area and parallel to the street, the lower areas of these walls can be seen, constructed of large blocks taken from the Hellenistic walls and in-filled above with massive, fluted column-drums (probably from an ancient temple building) laid on their sides in a row. The square central bolt-holes which linked the drums into columns are still visible. Perpendicular to this are the ruins of a mediaeval vaulted building which abutted the walls to the north. Directly to the south a

mediaeval windmill stands on top of the remains of the southeast corner-tower, marking what was the limit of the Byzantine enceinte. Below it on the south side is a row of three **Ottoman water-fountains**. The windmill is private property and cannot be visited; but another one, 100m to the west can be entered and provides a wide panorama of the city (*see below*).

Omírou Street

Omírou Street leads west from the row of three Turkish fountains, and passes to the right of what remains of the late 14th century church of SS. Theodore (*behind the doorway at right angles to the entrance of the 'Pension Minos'. Currently closed for restoration*). In a loop to the south of Omírou, is Aristeídou Street (its two ends being the 1st and 2nd turnings to the left off Omírou): it runs close to the inside of the south walls and brings you to a second **windmill**, whose parapet reached by the spiral staircase inside offers a comprehensive **view** over the Old Town. Immediately below it to the west is the picturesque, 15th century church of **Aghia Kyriakí**, set in a hollow shaded with palm-trees; the simple, barrel-vaulted interior has no paintings, but the church has preserved its minaret and *mihrab* from the period of its use as a mosque ('Borucan Mescid'). The next loop, to the south of Omírou, is that of Antísthenous Street. This leads into one of the quietest corners of the town and to the **church of St Michael**, standing in a pebbled *plateia* with an ilex tree and a small fountain composed of ancient *spolia* in front of its west entrance. The simple, apsed and barrel-vaulted building, is heavily buttressed on the north side; the stump of the minaret which was added in the 16th century is visible at the east end.

The Mosque of Recep Pasha

A gateway on the north side of Omírou Street leads through into the open area of Doriéos Square, shaded by mature *ficus* trees and dominated to the east by the most beautiful and architecturally interesting of the many mosques built by the Turks in the city—the ***Recep Pasha Cami** of 1588. What distinguishes it from the others are the beautifully proportioned forms of its gently rising profile and the fineness of its external decoration—never ostentatious, and always enhancing to the primary structure. Its form gives the pleasure of a unified piece of sculpture.

On the exterior viewed from the side are three levels of cornice-lines, each beautifully defined with simple moulding; the windows are articulated with carved arches, ornate at the lower levels, and sober at the top around the dome; the subtle passage from (the 16-sided) drum to circular dome is made manifest by a running polygonal cornice around its crown. More elaborate decoration is used only at the base of the broken minaret and around the imposing central doorway. The surface decorations of the interior (*currently closed for restoration*) include 16th century **Iznik tile panels** bearing Koranic verses in fine calligraphy; there are also painted panels of floral decoration above the windows, which use the colours and motifs of Iznik-ware. The building incorporates monolithic columns from earlier Christian structures. It is the work of an architect of considerable accomplishment. Above the door is the **dedicatory inscription** of Recep Pasha, expressing the justified wish that the space 'may inspire an uplifting of the spirit'.

The octagonal *shadirvan*, or **ritual fountain**, to the west has survived in good condition: overgrown with vegetation, to the east side, is the *türbe* or **mausoleum** of Recep Pasha—its windows embellished with the interlocking voussoirs typical of high, Ottoman architecture.

Aghios Phanoúrios and Athenas Square

The western exit of Doriéos Square leads into one of the best-preserved arteries of the mediaeval town—**Aghiou Phanoúriou Street** which follows the north/south line of a street of the ancient city. Its length is punctuated by bracing buttresses linking the buildings on either side of the street, giving them protection from tremors and earthquakes. To the south is the 13th century church of **Aghios Phanoúrios**—active and important before the arrival of the Knights, and still one of the most frequented churches of the city today. Beyond an unenticing, prefabricated metal and glass vestibule, the old church lies at considerably lower level—its numinous, domed interior entirely decorated with three successive layers of **wall-paintings** (13th, early 14th, and 15th century) in deteriorating condition, due to crystalline efflorescences and layers of smoke grease.

The most legible area (dated by an inscription to 1335/36—the years in which the western arm of the church appears to have been extended) is the niche on the right as you enter, showing the hatted benefactors or *donors and their wives presenting the church to Christ, in a garden of pomegranate trees. The ghostly forms of the Archangel Michael in the north transept and of the Pantocrator in the dome are visible; but many of the other scenes of the *Twelve Feasts* and of the *Life of the Baptist* on the vaults and walls are largely unreadable in their present condition. After so many closed churches in the town, the devotion which can be sensed here is refreshing. Aghios Phanoúrios is a popular local saint, about whose life virtually nothing is known. His cult goes back allegedly to the finding of an icon bearing his name and scenes of his martyrdom, probably around the 9th century. He is the patron saint of the finding of lost things, and it is traditional to dedicate a cake (a '*Phanourópita*') to the saint in thanks for items retrieved. He is a predominantly Rhodian saint, and the unbroken, centuries-old cult in this church is testimony to his considerable local importance.

Another of the city's churches which predates the arrival of the Knights, the 13th century **Aghios Spyridon**, lies 200m to the north, down the narrow alley-way opposite the Marco Polo Hotel. It is of an inscribed-cross plan, surmounted by a low cupola pleasingly decorated with a slightly uneven blind arcade. Its history is long and complex, as the extensive excavations being undertaken around and inside it are revealing. Outside the church, these have revealed fragments of antique columns, the ubiquitous stone projectiles, and sections of 6th century AD foundations below: inside, Early Christian sepulchral chambers and ancient masonry have been brought to light, suggesting that there may have been a funerary chapel on this site attached to the large basilica to the east (*see below*) in Early Christian times. The interior still conserves small areas of painting. The stocky minaret from the church's period as the 'Kavaklı Mescid' is perfectly preserved.

To the east of Aghios Spyridon, Athenas Square opens out, whose irregular area is the result of damage in the Second World War. It is bisected by the impressive ruins of the 14th century **basilica of the Archangel Michael**, which was perhaps built by the Greek community as a new cathedral after the Panaghia tou Kastrou (whose form it closely resembles) had been appropriated by the Knights. The excavations reveal to the north side the foundations of a large Early Christian basilica of the 6th century (part of the curve of the main apse protrudes to the north at the lowest level). This was destroyed perhaps as early as the 8th century; a small Byzantine church was then built over its south aisle, which survived until the larger 14th century church was built to replace it on the same site. This became the 'Demirli Cami' under the Turks, and was then irreparably damaged during the last war. The surrounding excavations reveal sections of wall, columns and segments of decorative frieze—some with exquisite bay-leaf design. Areas of painted decoration survive in the ruined apse of the Mediaeval building.

The Mehmet Agha Mosque

The northern extension of Aghiou Phanoúriou Street ends at right angles to the main market street (Sokrátous Street) below one of the city's most visible mosques, whose windows and wide wooden eaves overlook the street at a conspicuously different angle from everything else: this is the recently restored **Mehmet Agha Mosque**, built in two separate phases between 1820 and 1875. It is of a design which was generally used for crowded sites such as this; the prayer hall was raised well above a ground floor of arcaded shops, the rent from which contributed to the upkeep and charitable work of the mosque. The (restored) **minaret**, which here takes the form of a central, canopied, wooden tower above the main door, is of a design commoner in Syria and the Levant, and shows the eclecticism of Ottoman architecture in this twilight period. The three water fountains below, surmounted by marble plaques inscribed in Osmanli and dated 1291 (1874/5 in the Western calendar), are contemporary with the mosque.

The entire length of **Sokrátous Street** can be best appreciated from this point as it rises from the harbour to the Mosque of Suleiman which crowns its summit. The line of one of the most important streets of Ancient Rhodes lies below it. In Byzantine and Mediaeval times the street was more an open space and market area, with its north side being formed by the south walls of the fortress which can still be seen 30m to the north on Theophiliskou and Agesandrou Streets. Later, in Ottoman times, the area was built up thereby defining Sokrátous Street (then called 'Uzun Çarşı') as the main *bazaar* of the city.

*The **second loop** in this area begins a few metres to the west of the Agha Mosque, where Menekléous Street meets Sokrátous Street.*

Ariónos Square and the Mosque of Mustafa III

Menekléous Street winds through a succession of small squares lined with restaurants and cafés. On the right hand side (after the third dog-leg of the street) is the three-aisled **church of SS. Constantine and Helen**—inconspicuous, and yet one of the oldest surviving churches within the city. Once again excavations beneath the floor of the existing 12th century structure are revealing earlier building on the same site. The exterior base of the east wall incorporates several carved ancient fragments in white marble, including a finely wrought capital. The interior is mostly bare, but a small panel of late Byzantine wall-painting survives in the south east corner. A similar situation is encountered at **Aghios Artemios** (14th/15th century) in Ergiou Street (30m to the south), where vestiges of later painting still decorate the door-frame, and fragments of columns, bases and capitals in different coloured marbles are immured in the earlier walls and foundations around the church. It was not uncommon for a dedication to St Artemios to be used when a church replaced a pre-existing shrine to Artemis.

At its summit, Menekléous Street opens into Ariónos Square in front of the bulky form of the **Mosque of Mustafa III** (1765). The building is a shadow of its former self: it has lost its minaret, the wide, pillared porch which shaded the main door, and the canopy over its **finely carved fountain** in front. But some of its decoration still survives: an ornate inscription over the door (bearing the Sultan's dedication), and the *mimbar*, the *mihrab* and the wooden gallery inside the spacious prayer hall. Opposite the mosque are the buildings of the *****Yeni Hamam**, now carefully restored and functioning as **municipal baths** (*open Mon–Fri 10–5; Sat 8–5*). The earliest complex on the site was first built either under Suleiman the Magnificent or his successor Selim II in the years between 1558 and 1568 as a men's baths; in 1765 it was enlarged by Mustafa III with the addition of the women's baths. Together they constitute one of the finest examples of an Ottoman *hamam* outside of the three royal cities of Istanbul, Bursa and Edirne. In Rhodes, the baths perhaps lack the critical mass of bathers they would have in an Islamic city; but the interiors are constructed with fine materials and proportions, and they reward visiting. The main, domed entrance chamber is a beautiful space with a height equivalent to its diameter.

Ippodámou Street

From Ariónos Square, Acheláou Street leads north to Ippodámou (Hippodámou) Street, at a point almost opposite the 15th century church of **Aghia Paraskevi**. This is best seen from the courtyard in front of its west end, just off Xenophóntos Street, from where the fine Gothic portal as well as the church's profile and the pleasing relationship of cruciform plan to octagonal drum are most easily appreciated. Xenophontos Street continues further south, joining Alexandrídou Street at the **mosque of Hamza Bey** (*currently under restoration*). The building's design is pure and simple, following a classic sequence used in Ottoman mosques—a square (cubic) prayer-hall surmounted by a dome, articulated externally by an octagonal drum.

Further south on Ippodámou Street, the narrow entrance of Androníkou Street (signed to the 'Traditional Theatre') leads east down to the entrance of the 15th century, monastic complex of **St Nicholas**. (This is also

referred to, in different periods, as both **St Bernardin** and
St Augustine, and was known in Ottoman times as the
'Abdul Djelil Mescid'). The attractively walled and land-
scaped compound is entered through an ornate **doorway**, bordered by a carved rope-design and surmounted
by a framed niche, now lacking its dedicatory mural.

The present structure of the *catholicon*—two parallel vaulted
aisles joined by two wide arches—appears to have been built
over an Early Christian predecessor. The building was damaged during the last war, and its vaults have been restored:
small areas of late 15th century wall-painting with scenes
relating to the life of St Nicholas have been rescued from the
interior. The stump of the minaret remains to the west, and
the exterior shows evidence of a vaulted portico which once
extended from the south wall. Some of the monastic cells
survive to the south east of the church.

At the southern extremity of Ippodámou Street, in the
corner to the left facing the inside of the city walls, are the
remains of buildings from the **Roman** *Agora* of Rhodes.
The area is still too small to see clearly the context of what
has been uncovered. It is a sunken area, paved and backed
by an immaculately constructed stretch of limestone wall
in isodomic blocks with beautifully hand-worked surfac-

es. One block with an inscription in Greek is visible in the centre of the second row, and the column bases of a *stoa* form a line below. At a much later date, the circular base of a windmill has been built at a higher level. This is the only area to have been uncovered of an agora complex which in the original plan of the city must have stretched for a considerable distance to both east and west of this point.

The Gate of St Athanasius and the southern walls

Ippodámou Street then rejoins Omírou Street. To the right, beyond the 16th century **church of St Athanasius** on the left side, is the *St Athanasius Gate of the Tongue of Aragon—once again different in design from the other city gates and substantially reinforced in the aftermath of 1480 with a massive crescent bastion. Today the carriage-way passes through a narrow tunnel, turns right along a *fausse-braie* and then crosses over the deep moat onto the independent bastion. The ground far below is littered with projectiles. To the right is the original (pre-1480) circular **Tower of the Virgin**—which immediately seems vulnerable and antiquated by contrast with the later, pro-tecting, outer bastion. On its south face is a white marble **sculpture of the Virgin and Child** in an aedicule above the coats of arms of Grand Master Jean de Lastic and an inscription bearing the date 1441.

In 1501 the idea was mooted by Grand Master d'Aubusson of sealing the d'Amboise and St Athanasius Gates for security reasons: this was not done in the case of the former, but it appears that it was carried out with this gate. In September 1522 it was briefly re-opened for a sortie: by this time the walls in this sector had been reduced in places to rubble by Turkish mining and artillery fire. It appears that Suleiman the Magnificent first entered the city he had captured through the St Athanasius Gate, giving orders immediately afterwards that it be walled up so that nobody else might pass through it again. It was only reopened in 1922.

As you stand on the bridge, to the east side stretch the **inner walls of the sector of the Tongue of England** (previously of the Tongue of Aragon, until the two swapped positions before the siege of 1522), with a long *fausse-braie* linking a chain of towers down its length. In front, facing you at a distance of 20m, stands the blunt end of the long, independent advance-rampart which rises up from the bed-rock. Along the length of this sector the coats of arms of six Grand Masters (Fluviā, de Lastic, de Milly, Orsini, d'Aubusson and del Carretto) bear witness to the continuous campaigns of modification and improvement. Two hundred metres east down the walk along the facing counterscarp is the Gate of St John, beyond a small **Ottoman fountain**. The next (eastern) itinerary begins here.

EASTERN SECTOR: EAST OF PYTHAGORA STREET

The Gate of St John or 'Koskinou Gate'

At the **Gate of St John**, also called the '**Koskinou Gate**' (and sometimes locally, **Kokkino** ('Red') Gate), a high bridge leads across to the outer entrance, surmounted by the arms of the Order and of Grand Master Pierre d'Aubusson in an ornately **carved cornice** and steeply pointed pediment which forms a continuation of the string-course of the walls themselves. To either side diagonal lines in the masonry show where the tower was heightened and consolidated before 1522, and several blocked circular ports (originally cannon emplacements) can be seen in the parapet to the eastern side. The top of the parapet slopes markedly outward to deflect enemy missiles. The outer gate leads into an independent bastion, whose crescent plan completely shields the square **Tower of St John** at its centre. This is reached across a second, exposed bridge (now stone, but originally a wooden draw-bridge) leading to a second gate, with the chapel of St John the Baptist to the left. Above and to the left of the final gate ahead, and partially hidden by the low wall on the left (west) side, is a grey **marble plaque inscribed in both Italian and Greek** recording that in August 1457 this part of the walls was raised and re-built by one Manoulis Kountis, who describes himself as 'master-builder of all the new walls of Rhodes'. Turning back after passing under this inner gate into the city, you see the wooden beam into which the doors were fixed, still bearing the Islamic date 1202 (1787) of its restoration. The gate leads into a crowded area of popular houses and workshops: immediately to the left is an undecorated **sarcophagus**, still with its lid, formerly used as a water fountain. Opposite are the steps which are the usual exit for the walking-tour of the walls. The left-turn ahead leads into Pythagóra Street and the Central area of the Old Town: this itinerary turns east here, i.e to the right.

Holy Trinity Church (Aghia Triada) and St Catherine

The first turning left, shortly after Efthimíou Street passes under the arch of a building, is Nikíou Street. This leads past the minuscule 14th century church of **Aghia Marina** (right) into Leonidas Rodoiou Square—dominated to the west by the striking silhouette of the 15th century ***church of the Holy Trinity** (Aghia Triada) which rises above an area of fragrant bushes of jasmine, bougainvillea and hibiscus. (*open—purportedly—Tues–Sun 12.30–2.30*). A constantly varying roof-scape of different forms below a high octagonal drum, punctuated by a broken minaret with a beautifully dentillated '**collar**', suggests a complex history for the building which in the last phase saw its conversion into a mosque—the 'Dolaplı Mescid'. The building probably began as the *catholicon* of a monastic complex; it appears to have been extended to south and to west. It incorporates a square room in its north arm whose octagonal, rib-vaulted roof would suggest that it was used as a baptistery. (Eight-sided spaces and cupolas had been most commonly used for baptisteries since earliest times.)

Though humble in proportions, the building was once outstandingly decorated: the large, **ornate insets** of Latin-cross form, visible to either side of the north doorway, were once filled with ornamental ceramic tiles; the exquisite wooden doors, conserved today in the ground-floor exhibition '*Rhodes from the 4th century until the Turkish Conquest*' in the Grand Masters' Palace (*see p. 55*), came from this church; the west door has **carved ornamentation** above; the south wall contains fragments of ancient marble; the interior **floor** is laid with coloured marbles; and the walls decorated with interesting *****paintings**. The earliest paintings (figuring three bishops) are in the lunette on the east wall of the south arm. The others, of the later 15th century, include: *St Mary of Egypt receiving communion* (south arm); the *Deësis* and *Communion of the Apostles* in the east end; and a series of unusual *scenes from Genesis and Exodus* in the upper walls and vaults of the west arm—the *Expulsion from Eden*, *Cain and Abel*, and the *Flood* (in which the animals enter a Noah's ark which has more the appearance of a house than a sea-going vessel). These are paintings of an eclectic style, showing strong Western influence.

The square around the church has suffered considerable war damage; on the east side a house of some importance with 16th century, corniced windows has nonetheless survived. To its south, only 30m from Aghia Triada is the 14th century **church of St Catherine**, whose Turkish name 'Ilk Mihrab', meaning 'First Mihrab', suggests that this was the first place of Christian worship to be turned to Moslem use after the capture of the city in 1522. This is a small, architecturally unprepossessing church consisting of three contiguous barrel-vaulted aisles; but once again it is magnificently decorated with *paintings by 14th and 15th century artists of considerable accomplishment.

Particularly striking are the three figures of *Christ with the donor couple* above the entrance on the west wall—the husband presenting the church, the wife holding out a purse. The vigorous modelling of the figure of *St Peter* on the same wall shows the skill of the artist working here: though traditional in style, there is a freshness and lack of rhetoric, and an attention to the expressive use of colour. In the vault are the *Twelve Sacred Feasts* and scenes of the *Life of John the Baptist*; in the conch is the *Deësis*. All of these are late 14th century paintings. The series in the south aisle were painted perhaps a century later: these include the *Last Supper*; the *Hospitality of Abraham*; and scenes of the *Life of St Catherine*.

The area north and east of here was the city's **Jewish Quarter**, once the most vibrant and lively corner of the Old Town. The Jewish community today is drastically diminished in size by comparison with what it was before the purges of the last century. The area is now a mixed neighbourhood: its architecture is one of low, simple buildings of popular character, with projecting wooden balconies—very different in feel from the stately streets of the Collachium area. At the point where Gavalas Street meets the walls an area of deep excavation has revealed the remains of a building referred to as the '**Roman Triconch Building**'. Only one of the conches is clearly visible at the north end; the other two are just perceptible to south and east. This was probably a *nymphaeum*, or else part of a gymnasium and baths complex incorporating a *piscina*.

The eastern extremity of the Old Town

To the right after 50m is the **Acandia Gate** of the Tongue of Italy, protected to the south by the del Carretto Bastion, designed with angled embrasures and cannon-ports both at the parapet and at the level of the ground by Basilio dalla Scuola in 1517/18. This was always destined to be one of the more vulnerable points of the city's enceinte, because it is here that the moat levels out towards the coast. Suleiman was not blind to this fact and directed his most insistent artillery and cannon fire against this gate from the outset of the siege.

A short distance south along Kisthiníou Street on the left, is a **commemorative water-fountain** dedicated by the International Jewish Community in 1913 to General Giovanni Ameglio who took Rhodes for the Italians in May 1912, entering the city through the Jewish Quarter. He became the island's first commander and promoted largely respectful relations between the authorities and the Jewish community, which at that time numbered nearly 5,000 people.

The street ends in front of the busy, 15th century **church of St Panteleimon**, whose interior has been lavishly redecorated with modern, Byzantine paintings of some merit: these are not wall-paintings, however, but executed on linen affixed to the wall. This is similar to the method used by Venetian painters in the 16th century to circumvent the effects of damp on fresco, which gave momentum to the development of oil-on-stretched-canvas painting in Western art: it is curious to see history repeat itself here in the Byzantine tradition, 500 years later. Behind the church, against the eastern extremity of the walls, are the scant excavated remains of a large Gothic, rib-vaulted, single-aisled church dedicated by Pierre d'Aubusson to '**Our Lady of Victory**'. The church's life was short and poignant: built after the 1480 siege in thanks to the Virgin for salvation, it was destroyed again in the siege of 1522; its ruins suffered final destruction in the last War.

From this vantage point at the end of the town, the long line of the **Hellenistic harbour walls** can be seen stretching 100m westwards, their meticulously drafted blocks, set into the bed-rock defining two clear borders. At the point where the width of the archaeological area opens out after 50m, the line of the walls deflects slightly and the base of a circular fortification-tower behind them can be seen. At the opposite end, just before they are covered by the building of the Hospice of St Catherine, the transverse cut of a postern gate can also be detected. At their easternmost limit these walls formed a mole or breakwater extending around the harbour beyond the area of habitation.

The Hospice of St Catherine and the Church of St Mary of the Burgh

Straddling the line of the Hellenistic walls is the predominantly 15th century **Hospice of St Catherine**, built around a central courtyard and founded in 1392 by Fra Domenico d'Alemagna to give help and hospitality to Italian pilgrims travelling to and from the Holy Land. Parts of the building to either side are missing, but the surviving block has soberly decorated windows, a beautifully carved string-course, and projecting carved waterspouts at roof-level. The founders arms are visible on the north façade; those of Grand Master del Carretto and Admiral Costanzo Operti (whose mansion was encountered in Lachitos Street in the Collachium) on the west side. A little to the south is another large area of **excavations** which has revealed a cruciform church of relatively small dimensions, possibly also dedicated to St Catherine. Vestiges of the church's paintings can be seen low down amongst the walls which have been exposed. To the south, is an area of attractive *chochlakia* pavement belonging to a much later period.

Pindarou Street returns west, back towards the commercial area passing alongside the substantial remains of **St Mary of the Burgh**—roofless apart from a southwest chapel and the three gothic apses of the east end which still stand, with their long lancet windows and ribbed vaults. For most of the last century the site was bisected from north to south by the course of Alchádef Street: the street has since been closed and the nave of the church is now a theatrical setting for children to play among the column bases and for swallows to nest under the arches. Built according to a Western Gothic design by the Knights just after the middle of the 14th century, it comes in age and size shortly after its sister-church of St Mary of the Castle, from whom its epithet distinguishes it: the 'Castle' was the area of the Knights, while the 'Burgh', to the east, was the area of the commoners and merchants. The delicately carved decoration of foliage around the capitals between the apses, is complemented by the plants which grow from cracks in the masonry. From the church, the view through the gate breached in the walls directly to the north extends uninterrupted across the water to the mountains of Turkey.

The Synagogue and Catalan Mansion

Both of the two narrow streets (Byzantíou and Symmíou) west of St Mary of the Burgh lead into the heart of Jewish Rhodes and to the Synagogue. On the right hand side of Byzantiou, a doorway with a Hebrew inscription gives onto the roofless, vaulted ruin of what was once a synagogue ('Kahal Midrash'). During the last War, this area was the worst affected by British air-raids—just as it had been the area most damaged in the sieges of 1480 and 1522. Only about 40 Jews now remain on Rhodes and only one of the four synagogues and three oratories that once served the community survives—the **Kahal Kadosh Shalom** (or '**Congregation of Peace**') at no. 8 Symmíou Street. Built between 1575 and 1577, it is the oldest standing synagogue in Greece (*open daily, except Sat, 10.30–3*).

An elegant and luminous rectangular prayer-hall of fine proportions is traversed breadth-wise by two rows of stone columns and pure arches. The lay-out is typical of Sephardic synagogues, with the **Bema** or *Tevah*, in the centre of the room facing in the canonical direction of Jerusalem. The floor is attractively paved in Rhodian *chochlakia* work with an abstract design, and bears the date 5601 (1840). The walls were originally decorated with murals of the Ten Commandments: these have been partially—and a little clumsily—repainted on the left-hand wall. (The difference can be seen on entering between the decorative elements on the central arch which are original, early 19th century work, and those on the smaller arch to the right which are re-painted.) The collection box is a fluted, pagan altar-stand. To the east side of the building is a courtyard where a **water-fountain** has been recently uncovered bearing an inscription in Hebrew with the date 5338 (1577)—the same year as the completion of the synagogue.

THE JEWISH COMMUNITY OF RHODES

It was in the early years of Ottoman rule—one of the freest and most tranquil periods for the Jews in Greece—that the synagogue was built. Jews had been present in Rhodes since the 3rd or 2nd century BC, attracted by its commercial vitality; they are referred to by Suetonius a couple of centuries later; and in 12th century Byzantine Rhodes there was a community of over 500. Their co-existence with the Knights of St John was peaceful and constructive until, in the wake of the Spanish expulsion of Jews during the Inquisition, Grand Master Pierre d'Aubusson under pressure from the Church imposed either exile or forced conversion on the island's Jews in 1502. Most took advantage of the 40 day period of grace and left for Salonica, Ferrara, Constantinople and other destinations with already large Jewish populations. Suleiman the Magnificent, on taking the city, did more than rescind this proscription: he encouraged the repatriation of Jews to Rhodes, sanctioned a measure of administrative autonomy for them and accorded several privileges to the community. This attracted many Jews to Rhodes again, but the result was that the balance of the community changed: there were many more Sephardic refugees from Spain now settling in Rhodes than there were original, Greek-speaking Jews, and they brought with them a Judaeo-Spanish language referred to as 'ladino'. It was widely used right through into the 20th century: the newspaper of the community appeared in *ladino*. Italian occupation after 1912 initially brought no particular discrimination or problems under the Governorship of Mario Lago; but, with the arrival of Cesare Maria de Vecchi in 1936, restrictions increased and autonomy was successively reduced, until the Fascist racial laws finally enshrined the elimination of Jewry as an article of faith. The inevitable consequences of the island passing under Nazi German control in 1943 are dispassionately recounted in the small display in the rooms adjoining the Synagogue. In July 1944 almost 1,600 Jews who had not had the possibility or foresight to flee before were rounded up, shipped from Rhodes to Athens, and thence ultimately to Auschwitz. Only 30 men and perhaps 120 women survived; but the unbroken, millennial community of Jews on Rhodes was finished.

Across from the Synagogue, a little further up Symmíou Street, is a remarkable 15th century mansion referred to as the '**Catalan House**', because of the especially wide voussoirs of the arch of its **portal** which are characteristic of Late Mediaeval, Catalan building practice. The gate leads into a low entrance-court with a broad, sweeping vault above. Much of the upper area inside has gone, leaving only the façade standing. The **window frames** are delicately defined with oak-leaf and rosette motifs: these combined with the massive doorway below, give the building a noble air that is unexpected in such an area of simple residences. The unusual and ornate shape of its surround suggests that the small coat of arms on the façade of the building belonged to a more recent owner.

The house of the Greek Bishop

Pindarou Street leads into what was known to the Jewish community as the 'Calle Ancha' ('Broad Street')—the heart of the Judería—renamed today the '**Square of the Hebrew Martyrs**' in memory of those who died in the Holocaust. The pleasant square, surrounded by balconied buildings, occupies the area of a mediaeval square named after another martyr of persecution—St Sebastian. The north side is dominated by the fine, 16th century '**house of the Greek Bishop**' (sometimes arbitrarily referred to as the '**Admiralty**'). It is certainly a noble building; but the hypothesis that it was an arch-episcopal residence is based solely on the two inscriptions—one in Latin on the façade, the other in Greek above the stairs inside—which both read 'Peace be with this house and all who dwell in it'. The importance of the mansion is emphasised by the ornate **window-frames** and the decisive moulding of the **string-course** which divides the functional ground floor of vaulted store-rooms from the elegant and perfectly symmetrical *piano nobile* above. From the fountain in front of the building, Aristotelous Street leads west back to Ippokrátous Square—the hub of the commercial life of the walled city.

RHODES: THE NEW TOWN AND AREAS OUTSIDE THE WALLS

THE AQUARIUM

The esplanade of the Rhodes Aquarium at the **northernmost tip of the island** looks out as if from the prow of a ship towards the steep mountains of Turkey which line the horizon across the water: ahead, to the right, is the sea-route to Cyprus, Egypt and the Levant; to the left is the main route north through the islands up to Byzantium and the Black Sea. This stretch of water was the turning-point on one of the most important commercial trading routes of Antiquity: hence the decision to found the city of Rhodes here. Looking back towards the south, the long, flat table-top hill of the acropolis of Ialysos, with the central mountains of the island behind, can be seen. In the foreground is Mount Smith, the ancient Acropolis of Rhodes—also flat-topped—with its steep slope to the western seaward side. Towards the southeast is a pleasing assemblage of Italian buildings of different forms which extend in the direction of Mandraki harbour: this is the monumental heart of what is referred to as the 'New Town'.

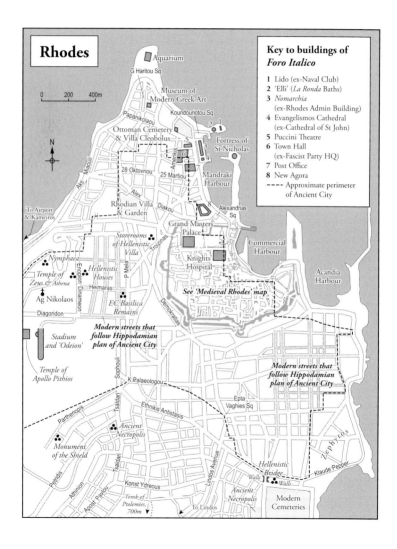

Rhodes

0   200   400m

N

Aquarium

G Haritou Sq

Museum of
Modern Greek Art

Papanikolaou   Koundouriotou Sq

Ottoman Cemetery
& Villa Cleobolus   5

Fortress of
St Nicholas

Amerikis

28 Oktovriou   25 Martiou

Mandraki
Harbour

Akti Miaouli

Alex
Diakou

Rhodian Villa
& Garden

To Airport
& Kameiros

Alexandrias
Sq

Grand Masters
Palace

Storerooms
of Hellenistic
Villa

Commercial
Harbour

Nymphaea

Trozmas

Enoplon Dinameon

P Mela

Knights
Hospital

Acandia
Harbour

Temple of
Zeus & Athena

Hellenistic
Houses

Heimaras

See 'Medieval Rhodes' map

Ag Nikolaos

Diagoridon

EC Basilica
Remains

Demokratias

Stadium
and 'Odeion'

*Modern streets that
follow Hippodamian
plan of Ancient City*

Temple of
Apollo Pithios

Sophouli

*Modern streets that
follow Hippodamian
plan of Ancient City*

K Palaeologou

Ethnikis Antistasis

Epta
Vaghies Sq

Tsaldari

Parthenopis

*Ancient
Necropolis*

Lindos Avenue

*Monument
of the Shield*

Tsaldari

Zephyros

Petrois

Athinion

Apost Pavlou

Konst Ydreous

*Hellenistic
Bridge*
Walls

Klaude Pepper

Walls

*Tomb of
Ptolemies,
700m*

To Lindos

*Ancient
Necropolis*

Modern
Cemeteries

Key to buildings of
Foro Italico

1 Lido (ex-Naval Club)
2 'Elli' (*La Ronda* Baths)
3 *Nomarchia*
      (ex-Rhodes Admin Building)
4 Evangelismos Cathedral
      (ex-Cathedral of St John)
5 Puccini Theatre
6 Town Hall
      (ex-Fascist Party HQ)
7 Post Office
8 New Agora
- - - - Approximate perimeter
      of Ancient City

The ***Aquarium** itself is one of the most pure and memorable buildings of the later period of the Italian Occupation. Its deliberately rounded corners and low, circular lantern underscore its position as the island's 'full-stop' or 'point of departure'. The simple, plain façade is relieved only by the blue and white reliefs of sea-creatures around the doorway, just as in the buildings raised by the Knights an often plain façade is relieved only by a highly ornate door-frame. The paving of the approach is lined with inset, ceramic medallions figuring the symbols of the various islands of the Dodecanese. The building was designed by Armando Bernabiti (*see box below*) and put up in 1934; both its proportions and the unity of its design are pleasing. It houses the city's interesting **Marine Aquarium and Hydrobiological Institute** (*open daily 1 Apr–31 Oct 9– 8.30; 1 Nov–31 March 9–4.30*).

The collection, which is mostly laid out below sea-level underneath the building, consists of an artificial, labyrinthine grotto of sea-water tanks containing a wide variety of local marine life, fish, crustaceans and reptiles (turtles), where it is possible to admire the variety of their forms and the extraordinary grace and sensitivity of their movements. The upper floor has a number of unusual preserved specimens, and some interesting marine exhibits visible through microscopes. The remarkable display of an *ancient monk-seal burial**, dating from the 1st century BC, is unique in what it tells us of ancient attitudes to animals: the seal's remains, together with small grave gifts, and the remains of humans and of a dog (also given funerary honours), were found ritually buried in a family inhumation which came to light during excavations in the area of the Commercial Harbour in 1999.

TWENTIETH CENTURY ITALIAN 'COLONIAL' ARCHITECTURE IN RHODES

For a long time neglected because of its unfortunate political connotations, the astonishing variety of buildings put up by the Italians during their occupation of the Dodecanese from 1912 to 1943, has been neither studied nor appreciated in proportion to its artistic merit. The Italians, who were late arrivals on the modern stage of Empire-building by comparison with the British or the French, sought to give a unifying architectural stamp to the Mediterranean and African territories which they occupied. At first they created a new, pan-Mediterranean, 'Rationalist' architecture which, by incorporating different elements of local traditions—Roman, Crusader, Ottoman, Greek, Islamic etc.—was intended to give the visible impression of the extent and diversity of Italy's new empire. This gave rise to the period's greatest and most imaginative buildings. But it was to prove a short-lived architectural 'spring': after 1936, with a new political Governor and the declaration of the Fascist 'Imperium', architecture had to bend to the demands for monumentality imposed by more regressive and authoritarian politics. Some of the earlier buildings were even purged of their decorative elements in a 'purification' of the colonial architecture. Fortunately, many more of the early buildings have survived throughout the Dodecanese than the later 'purified' ones. The juxtaposition of the two, seen at certain points in the New Town, is starkly revealing.

The two phases correspond to the periods in office of the two longest-serving Italian governors of the Dodecanese, both of whom were actively interested in architecture, but who held opposing views: the more moderate Mario Lago (1924–36), and his successor, Cesare Maria de Vecchi (1936–41), who had formerly been Mussolini's Minister for Education. It was Mario Lago who was responsible for the creation

of Porto Lago on Leros, for the rebuilding of Kos after the disastrous earthquake of 1933, for promoting
archaeological excavations on Rhodes and Kos, and
for the commissioning of a comprehensive new Master Plan for the expansion of the city of Rhodes outside the walls, which was entrusted to the architect
Florestano di Fausto and was approved already by
1926. The Master Plan envisioned the development
of an area—already partially used by the Turks for
administrative buildings and large residences—to
the west of the port of Mandraki, between the Old
City and the northern tip of the island. Against the
theatrical backdrop of the City of the Knights, with
all its convenient associations of a Western, 'Latin'
dominance, a new *Foro Italico* of commercial and administrative buildings was to be spaciously laid out
along the shore. Associated with this plan for the city
was the wider project for the building of new streets
and roads, and the creation of numerous agricultural
settlements ('San Benedetto'/Kolymbía, 'San Marco'/
Aghios Pavlos, etc.) and resorts for *villeggiatura*
('Campochiaro'/Eleoúsa), at different points around
the island.

The architecture of **Florestano di Fausto** was highly eclectic. It grafted decorative elements from a variety of origins—Moorish domes, Venetian tracery, Gothic arches, and the clear, cuboid volumes of Aegean indigenous building—onto the framework of simple geometric forms favoured by 'Rationalist' architecture. It alternates in overall effect between a Crusader military purity at one extreme and an Oriental luxury at the other. Its most characteristic and architecturally courageous feature is the 'submerged' arcade—a broad, generally Gothic arch, or series of arches, supported on very low, stunted columns, which give the impression of having sunk into the ground. The effect is not unpleasing, and accentuates breadth and horizontality over the soaring height customarily associated with the Gothic arch. The origin of this idea lies in the *broglio*, or lower arcade, of the Doge's Palace in Venice; but it is much exaggerated when it reappears in the port-side arcade of di Fausto's Rhodes Administration (today's *Nomarchía*) Building of 1927. The other architects who worked in this period, such as **Rodolfo Petracco** and **Pietro Lombardi**, created buildings in a similar, if slightly purer architectural language. Lombardi's design for the Baths at Kallithea is perhaps the most unified masterpiece of the whole movement.

With **Armando Bernabiti**, there is a transition to a new generation of building in the late 1930s— purer, undecorated, and in every way more minimal and more consonant with the politics of the repressive Governorship of Cesare Maria de Vecchi. The simplicity is recognisable already in his early (1934) Aquarium building; but his later creations—the Puccini Theatre, the Rhodes Town Hall (formerly the *Casa Littoria*, or Fascist Administration Building), and the church of St Francis—all tend ineluctably toward the military in spirit. It was in this later period that a number of di Fausto's earlier buildings, such as his once extravagant *Albergo delle Rose*, were 'purified' of their decorative details and 'arabesques' to reveal a stern, more serious, core in unadorned '*poros*' limestone.

MUSEUM OF MODERN GREEK ART

The elongated, elliptical square directly to the south of the aquarium (officially named Plateia Gabriel Haritos, after the first Mayor of Rhodes), is lined with young palm-trees which replace the original ones planted during the Italian Occupation, after which the square took its commoner name, 'Square of the Hundred Palms'. The square, with eight radiating streets, was part of the New Urban Plan for Rhodes drawn up in 1926 aimed at developing a new administrative and residential area to the north of the Old City. In a large building on the eastern side of the square is the **Museum of Modern Greek Art** which incorporates the collection of the former 'Art Gallery of Rhodes' (*open Tues–Sat 8–2, Fri also open 5–8*).

The collection is well displayed over two floors: the first floor dedicated to Masters of 19th and 20th century Greek Art, and the upper floor to Contemporary painting in Greece. The first shows the constant tension within early modern Greek painting between those who worked within a European (predominantly French-influenced) academic tradition on the one hand, and the voice of a more distinctly Greek, 'folk' tradition, often of a consciously *naïf* character, on the other. Notable amongst the first group are: two striking portraits (one of the novelist, Alexander Papadiaman-tis) by **Photis Kontoglou**—creator of the wall-paintings in the Metropolitan Church of the Annunciation by Mandraki harbour; several nature studies and **landscapes** by Lytras, Thomopolis, Ghyka and Maleas; and some more specifically Rhodian landscapes by Valias Semertzidis. Among the sec-ond group are: *par excellence*—a number of historical paint-ings by **Theophilos**, as well as his more lyrical *Erotokritos and Aretousa*; a series of unusual and technically interest-ing, Byzantinizing pieces of the 1940s by **Spyros Vasiliou**, in tempera on paper with accompanying poetic texts in beauti-ful calligraphy; and three whimsical figure-studies by **Yannis Tsarouchis** from successive periods of his development.

Several of the most prominent and distinctive artistic per-sonalities of contemporary Greek Art—**Alekos Fassianós** and **Yannis Gaïtis**—are represented on the upper floor. But, although a bold variety of techniques is represented among the other recent works exhibited on this floor, the tendency towards abstraction has inevitably meant a loss of recogniz-ably Greek identity.

THE 'GRAND ALBERGO DELLE ROSE' (CASINO) AND THE AREA OF THE OTTOMAN CEMETERY

South down Kos Street from the aquarium is the large building of the ***Grand' Albergo delle Rose***, which today also incorporates the city's casino. First designed by Florestano di Fausto in 1925 as an orientalising Grand Hotel in the Levantine style, the building was later stripped of its external decoration in 1938 in the prevailing change of political rhetoric coming from the Fascist government in Rome: the ornate arch around the apse on the chamfered southwest corner, which was closely based on the ornate arches of the west front of St Mark's in Venice, was eliminated. In the grounds are the remains of a windmill. Just beyond the southern exit of the hotel is the tiny ***Villa Cleobolus***, where Lawrence Durrell lived from May 1945 until April 1947, and composed the greater part of his *Reflections on a Marine Venus*. 'It is difficult to convey the extraordinary silence of this garden', he wrote referring to the dense vegetation in the picturesque **Ottoman cemetery**, a corner of which the minuscule villa occupies. The large area of the cemetery is shaded with eucalyptus trees and encompasses today several domed mausolea or *türbe*, and a multitude of inscribed tombstones, many with carved turbans. In the 15th century, however, it was occupied by a cemetery of the Knights and a walled garden belonging to the Grand Master. Cecil Torr recounts that the garden was said to contain a number of strange animals, including a family of ostrich who fed on iron and steel and having laid their eggs in the sand, hatched them simply by looking at them.

The entrance to the cemetery is at its eastern extremity, through a doorway on the west side of Koundouriótou Square. A passage between two fine Ottoman houses in perilous state of conservation leads into a pebble-paved courtyard where the Turkish guardian and his family still live. The 19th century mosque (left), with its **ornate minaret** in Egyptian style, still functions; it is built on the site of the former Hospitaller church of St Anthony. The *türbe* to the right contains the green-draped sarcophagus of a 16th century corsair, Murat Reis, who became admiral under Suleiman the Magnificent and played an important role in the elimination of piracy from Ottoman waters. He died in 1609 and his tomb is respectfully maintained as a place of cult. Beneath the trees beyond these buildings, the domed structures (mostly eight sided) of mausolea—which include those of a Safavid Shah of Persia, and of a Tartar Prince—have remarkably managed to survive intact, although the sarcophagi inside have mostly been ransacked. Given the Prophet Mohammed's clear injunctions on the simplicity of funerary monuments, the fineness of these *türbe* is a measure of the importance of the figures they commemorate.

To the south across Papanikoláou Street from the cemetery, in front of the side of the Theatre, are substantial remains of **Hellenistic walls** constructed of enormous, meticulously cut limestone blocks: these constituted the northernmost projection of the walls, running from the eastern side of the entrance to the Military Harbour (today's 'Mandraki') across to a small western harbour which indented the coast in the area now occupied by the hotels to either side of the western end of Papanikoláou Street. To their south was possibly a sanctuary of Demeter. Many of the modern residential buildings in this area (such as the *Café Cavaliere* opposite) have the rounded corners, horizontal lines, and circular windows, typical of the architectural vocabulary of the Italian plan.

KOUNDOURIOTOU SQUARE, THE RHODES ADMINISTRATION BUILDING AND THE CATHEDRAL

***Koundouriótou Square** is a rich assemblage of some of the most interesting architecture of the Italian period. On the landward (west) side, the low wall of the cemetery (punctuated by a fine, carved Ottoman fountain, 10m to the north of the cemetery entrance) joins two early buildings by Florestano di Fausto: the **Naval Administration Building** (1925) to the south, with ornate window- and door- frames imitating those of the architecture of the Knights, and a unique, interwoven basket-work design in the plaster on the lower areas; and to the north, the **Rhodes Garrison Building** (1926), whose fine **monumental doorway** dominating the façade is directly inspired by elements of the Doge's palace in Venice. Opposite (north side of the square) is the large pantheon-like dome of the '**Elli**' building (1935: now a café and formerly 'La Ronda Sea Baths' complex) whose bolder, undecorated surfaces and purer geometric forms are typical of the work of Armando Bernabiti. The magnificent domed interior space is enlarged by an open surrounding ambulatory offering unencumbered glimpses of the open sea. Towards the shore (east side) is Rodolfo Petracco's **Lido** building of 1929 (formerly the Navy Club) with an extravagantly oriental silhouette, and an entrance decorated with relief mouldings of marine creatures and an anchor.

Closing off the square to the south is the most ornate of the four different façades of the '**Rhodes Administration Building**' (the *Nomarchía*, or Prefecture today) dating from 1926/7 by Florestano di Fausto. Although designed to be the centrepiece of the original *Foro Italico*, this is a highly idiosyncratic building, exhibiting many peculiarities of design and with something of an unresolved crisis of architectural identity. The arcade and its supporting columns are almost exaggeratedly 'submerged' here: the arches are of pointed, Gothic form at the north end and become almost immediately rounded and 'Rationalist' along the eastern front. The depth of the building is also precariously narrow in relation to its length. The short north façade is in a highly ornate, Venetian Gothic style, with extensive use of stone tracery; the long west façade is in severe Hospitaller idiom; and the east, port-side façade is a Rationalist meditation on the waterside front of the Doge's Palace in Venice, whose brick-work patterns are deliberately mimicked here. The resulting amalgam is not unsuccessful, but comes at considerable cost to stylistic coherence. The character of all these buildings is in total contrast to the severe '*Teatro Puccini*' of a decade later, which can be glimpsed just beyond to the southwest.

At its southern end, the 'Rhodes Administration Building' is linked by means of an open **Flag Court** to the Offices of the Metropolitan of Rhodes, which in turn is contiguous with the city's cathedral. The court is a wide-arched space, framing open views of the harbour and enclosing a ceremonial flag-pole mounted inside a well-preserved 2nd century AD, **Roman altar** in white marble decorated with *bucrania* and garlands: the borders of the broad spans of its arches are richly decorated with carved motifs in Hospitaller style. Di Fausto's two ecclesiastical buildings, projected in 1924 and completed in 1929—the former **Archbishop's Residence** (Offices of the Metropolitan) and the Cathedral of St John (now the **Metropolitan Church of the Annunciation**)—strike a rather dour note by comparison. The cathedral (which is curiously oriented on a north south axis) was created as a faithful recreation of the Hospitaller church of St John which once stood across from the Castle of the Grand Master and was destroyed in 1856; its exterior was originally spare and its interior undecorated, as befitted a military church. Once it became an Orthodox place of worship after 1947, a complete cycle of wall-paintings, in traditional Orthodox iconography, was commissioned for the interior. The painter, Photis Kontoglou (1895–1965) from Aivali in Greek Asia Minor, had always possessed artistic sympathies close to Byzantine subjects (see also his other works in the Museum of Modern Greek Art). The cycle includes the scenes of the *Life of Christ*, and of the *Life of Mary* according to the 24 verses of the Acathist Hymn.

ALONG THE WATER-FRONT OF MANDRAKI FROM THE DEMARCHEION BUILDING TO THE NEW AGORA

As you move inland to the west, across from the 'Rhodes Administration Building' into the **Square of the Demarcheion**, you observe a complete sea-change in the spirit of the architecture. The uncompromising volumes and geometric shapes of the 'Rationalist' canon are now more brutal; there is no colour, no decoration, no variety of texture. The square is formed by the *Demarcheion* or town hall of Rhodes (formerly the Fascist Headquarters), flanked (left) by the Police Building (the ex-Italian Military Administration) and (right) by the **Municipal Theatre** (formerly the *Teatro Puccini*). The design of these monolithic buildings vividly reflects the spirit of the new administration of Governor Cesare Maria de Vecchi (1936–41) and the increasing authoritarianism of Fascist rule in Rome in the period of his tenure. The buildings, created solely (and deliberately) from the same '*poros*' stone that was used by the Knights, are among the grimmest creations of Armando Bernabiti. The most interesting building of the group is the theatre, whose constant play of cylindrical and cuboid volumes evokes the walls, gates and bastions of the military architecture of the Knights.

South of the *Demarcheion* square, most of the line of buildings that face the harbour which were erected under the Governorship of Mario Lago have suffered the 'purifying' attentions of the de Vecchi administration. A notable exception is the main **post office**, designed by Florestano di Fausto in 1927/8 in a more straightforwardly classicising, 'Renaissance Revival' style: its grand order of engaged pilasters and pronounced window pediments must have been considered sufficiently dignified by de Vecchi not to require purging. In the large roundels in the attic, to either side of the Rhodian Helios in the centre, are symbols of the principal settlements of the island. Further south, the Port Authority building (formerly the *Casa del Fascio*) and the **Courthouse**, were both stripped of decorative content in 1938/9 and were transformed into close relations architecturally of the *Demarcheion* and the Theatre. The Courthouse sports protruding and unadorned, semicircular pilasters with neither capital nor base. By contrast, the **building of the Bank of Greece** (1931–33), formerly the Bank of Italy, by Biagio Accolti Gil, has a white marble base and an alternation of plastered areas and stone areas in its façade which does much to relieve the severity of its design.

Based on elements in the Mosque of Quairouan in Tunisia, the unmistakable, orientalising cupolas and arches of the **New Agora** (1925/6) at the southern extremity of the promenade has remained unmodified in the more capricious spirit of early Italian colonial architecture: its bold and imaginative design is typical of Florestano di Fausto's work. The entrance gateway facing the port is embellished with pleasingly decorated volutes supporting the arches. At the centre of the leafy and spacious interior is the raised fish-market kiosk with the original *scagliola* counters and water fountain under a cupola.

Scattered throughout the modern area of the New Town to the west, a number of shops, houses and offices in similar architectural vocabulary still survive from the same Master Plan. In Plateia Zygdis (three blocks inland from the Courthouse) is the Boy Scouts Centre, formerly the Fascist Youth Building (*Casa Balilla*) designed jointly by Lombardi and Bernabiti in 1932. Its concave façade has several unusual, Mannerist features, and an interesting decorative vocabulary of volutes and blind arches. In the same area (25th March Street) are a few well-preserved neoclassical villas. Underneath everything lies the ancient city, which reveals itself occasionally in sections of wall (Amerikis St.) or stretches of well-preserved ancient drains, built with arched stone covering (e.g. in front of the *National Bank of Greece*: west side of Kyprou Sqaure).

MANDRAKI HARBOUR

Mandraki—the more northerly of the city's two natural harbours—was the Military Port of the Ancient city, and later the principal ship-building yard of the Mediaeval city. The long mole, crowned with three ruined 17th century windmills which forms its eastern side is the result of a continuous enlargement of the original 4th century BC harbour walls along the same line. At its tip, the strategically important **Fortress of St Nicholas** (*currently closed to visits*) was built in the mid 1460s. It constituted the only forward bastion of the city's defences to the north and was vital for the protection of the two harbours. It proved its worth by effectively repulsing two successive Turkish onslaughts during the siege of 1480, and was re-fortified and enlarged afterwards against the next Turkish attack. The crenellated circular tower in the centre together with the lower, south-facing, additional stirrup-tower constitute the 15th century core, while the elliptical enceinte of walls around, with pronounced batter on the harbour side, were added as part of the early 16th century re-fortification. The whole structure was then repaired and modified in Ottoman times.

To its west, the entrance to the harbour is marked by two columns supporting bronze statues of a stag and a doe, symbols of the City of Rhodes. It is here that folk-tradition holds that the **Colossus of Rhodes** once stood, although it appears more likely that it was the largest of a group of smaller statues erected either in the southwest corner of the harbour, where the New Agora now stands, or else slightly further to the southwest, on the natural rise now occupied by the Palace of the Grand Masters.

THE COLOSSUS OF RHODES

It was a common practice in the Ancient world to dedicate a magnificent votive statue from the captured booty of a victorious campaign: the colossal bronze statue of Athena *Promachos* on the Acropolis in Athens was partly made with bronze captured at the Battle of Marathon. In this same spirit, the proceeds from the sale of the weapons and material left behind when Demetrios Poliorcetes lifted his failed siege of the city of Rhodes in 304/3 BC—estimated at 300 talents by Pliny (*Hist. Nat.* XXXIV, 18, 41/42)—was put to the making of a bronze statue of Helios, the patron divinity of the island. It was ceremonially dedicated to the god with due pomp at the five-yearly celebration of the pan-Hellenic festival of the *Halieia*. Though later merged in Greek cult with Apollo,

Helios long remained an independent divinity in
certain geographic areas, especially in the east of the
Greek world, as here on Rhodes. Chares of Lindos, a
student of Lysippus (who had already created a colossal bronze figure of Zeus for the city of Tarentum)
and who was one of the greatest bronze-working
sculptors of Antiquity, was given the commission for
the work—a task which led him eventually to bank-
ruptcy and suicide, according Sextus Empiricus.

The hollow statue, cast in many sections and laboriously assembled over an armature of metal rods
and masonry, stood to a height of around 32m (105ft)
and took 12 years to complete. Gilded sun-rays burst
from around the god's head, and, according to some
versions, he may have held a flaming torch in his
raised arm which functioned as a beacon to mariners. The figure was nude but for a shoulder-cloak.
Less than 60 years after its completion an earthquake in 227 BC sundered it at its most fragile point,
namely the lower legs. An oracular pronouncement
apparently forbad the citizens to re-erect it. It still lay
felled almost 250 years later in the time of Strabo and
Pliny—*sed iacens quoque miraculo est*, 'still a marvel

as it lies on the ground', according to the latter. Pliny says that it was hardly possible for a man to join arms around the thumb, and in the statue's carvernous interior could still be seen the material used to steady and support it. He goes on to mention that there were 100 other, smaller colossal statues in Rhodes.

The statue's bronze was eventually sold as scrapmetal in the Levant to Jewish traders in the 7th century AD, and no piece verifiably belonging to it has ever been seen since. Because the writer known as 'pseudo-Philo of Byzantium' included the Colossus in his 'Seven Wonders of the World', the vanished work excited great curiosity in Mediaeval times and was recreated in popular imagination impressively, but improbably, bestriding the entrance to the harbour. The Colossus of Rhodes may indirectly have been a model for the nude, bronze colossus of almost identical dimensions which Nero erected in Rome on the Velian Hill (until it was moved by Hadrian), and from which the Flavian Amphitheatre later was to take its better-known name, the 'Colosseum'. Nero's colossus was a portrait of himself as Helios, similarly crowned with sunrays radiating from the head.

ANCIENT RHODES—OUTSIDE THE CITY CENTRE

The **ancient city of Rhodes**, according to Strabo (*Geog.* XIV 2. 9), had been laid out on a plan drawn up by the 'architect of the Piraeus', namely Hippodamus of Miletus. It occupied a terrain which was neither steep nor confined by problematic geographical features, nor previously inhabited to any significant degree. Because the territory was ample, the city was planned spaciously. Its original core stretched in a wide, sloping band west from the Commercial Harbour and Acandia Bay to the summit of the acropolis (today's Mount Smith), which was crowned with large temples—to Apollo, Artemis, Zeus, Athena and other divinities. As the city rapidly grew in wealth and population it expanded both northwards in the direction of the point of the island and to the southeast, into the area occupied today by Zephyros. It was approximately 3km from the northern limit to the walls in the southeast. The 4th century southern walls run east along a course which cuts diagonally through the blocks south of today's Konstantinou Palaeologou and Garivaldi Streets, across the junction of Plateia Epta Vaghies, and then follow Grigoriou Vth Street and Klaude Pepper Avenue down to the shore along the north side of the main modern cemetery. Beyond this line, to the south, extended the ancient cemeteries.

In the area outside the mediaeval walled city, there are countless points where small elements of the Ancient break through the urban fabric of the Modern city. The most significant of these are mentioned below in two groups: the first in the area between the New Town and the ancient acropolis (Mount Smith); the second in the areas further to the south and east occupied predominantly by the ancient cemeteries. Most are of primarily academic interest, but three stand out as having a wider appeal: 1. the area of the upper acropolis and the *nymphaea* to its north; 2. the remains of the Early Christian basilica on Heimáras Street; and 3. the two decorated Hellenistic tombs—the so-called 'Tomb of the Ptolemies' and the 'Monument of the Shield'.

BETWEEN THE NEW TOWN AND THE ACROPOLIS

- The pleasing oasis of the **Rhodian Villa and Cultural Centre** (*open Mon–Fri 8.30–2.30, 3.45–9; Sat 7.45–1. Gardens open always in daylight hours*) stands in a mature garden in the heart of the one of the busiest areas of the town (access from both Diakou and Venizelou Streets). The institu-

tion houses a library and exhibition areas in a handsome
neoclassical villa with verandahs, surrounded by dense and
varied vegetation.

- The **storage rooms of a Hellenistic house** give an unusual
picture of the service areas and cellars of a 4th century BC
house. (*Entered to the left side of the large Tourism School
building on Troizinas Street, across from the d'Amboise Gate.
The site is at the far side of the car parking area, and lies
currently underneath a school building.*) Steps at first lead
down to the ancient floor-level, where there are two areas
of polychrome floor decoration, suggesting a residence of
some importance. Beside this and below, are several deep
chambers cut into the bed-rock used for storing grain and
other perishables. Insets for the original roof-beams can
be seen, as well openings for ventilation. The easternmost
chamber has small steps leading into it and grooves for
sliding a wooden retaining door; there are wedge-shaped
shafts at various points, used as chutes for filling the chambers. At the opposite end is a deep cylindrical well with
foot-holes to each side inside. In an age before refrigera-
tion and running water, these were the practical arrangements necessary for supplying a residence.

- The **Early Christian basilica** which lies beneath the buildings at the intersection of Heimáras Street and Pavlou Melá Streets, about half way up the acropolis hill, is the most extensive and important Palaeochristian complex uncovered in the city. The site is unattractively overhung with several apartment buildings which rise on concrete piles from the excavations; but the area uncovered and the quality of the exceptional *mosaic floor with abstract design (visible from Melá St.) still *in situ*, make it worth seeking out. In the southeast corner are remains of earlier antique paving and architectural elements. One block further west, along the edge of Sophouli Street, are the foundations of the street-facing façades of Hellenistic houses. The streets in this area closely follow the grid of the ancient Hippodamian plan.

- Nearby on the upper eastern slope of Mount Smith are the excavations of a so-called '**Palatial Building**' and of a **Hellenistic house**, which lie to either side of Enoplon Dinaneon Street. In the latter, below the level of a peristyle and pebble-mosaic floor can be seen a plastered, multiple-chambered cistern, suggesting an *impluvium* for water storage. Mosaic floor and elements of the water management system of a large residence can be seen in the 'Palatial Building' excavations.

•   The area of olive and oak trees stretching to the west of Di-
    agoridon Street and up to the crown of the hill is an **Ar-
    chaeological Park** (*always open*) comprising the Ancient
    Stadium, an (?) Odeion and the Temple of Pithian Apollo,
    most of which was first uncovered by Italian archaeologists
    between 1919 and 1929. According to the fashion of their
    time and the wishes of their political masters, what was un-
    covered was also considerably restored in a manner that has
    inevitably deadened its antique appeal. The ground level in
    and around the (2nd century BC) **Stadium** has risen leaving
    the first row of seats partly sunken: a gentle swelling curve in
    the line of two long sides can be detected. At the points where
    steps descend through the seating, small slots can be seen in
    the row of seats with back-rests, for the fixing of wooden
    retaining panels or doors. Beyond its north end, is a small
    building generally referred to as a 'theatre', which has been
    mostly reconstructed (apart from the orchestra and three
    of the seats, which are original). Although too small for a
    theatre proper, this probably functioned as an **Odeion**—a
    type of building designed for more intimate performances
    of music, song or poetry, as well as for teaching and occa-
    sional political meetings. The fact that the external form of
    the structure is square brings to mind the design of the '*bou-
    leuterion*', or council chamber, in Ancient Priene (Turkey)—
    a city which was also laid out by Hippodamus.

From the Odeion, steps lead up an impressive work of **terracing**. The Italian restorers have intervened heavily, but the well-designed stepping of some of the lower areas and the rustication of the ancient blocks clearly distinguish the antique work from the new. At the top, the ground flattens out onto the terrace of the twin-**sanctuary of Apollo Pithios,** and of his sister **Artemis**, whose temple stood below and a little to the north. The columns of one corner of the 4th century BC Temple of Apollo have been re-built by the Italian archaeologists to indicate the height of the building: it was a hexastyle Doric temple, oriented due east. The construction of its platform presents many points of interest: the floor of the interior *naos* was constituted by the cut, living bedrock; and the podium or *crepidoma* of the temple was created by cutting away the rock all around and then facing it with steps. These steps demonstrate the fine qualities of Hellenistic masonry, which is never lacking in pleasing details: the lowest step is rough-course bed-rock, the second step has a raised lip on its outer edge, and the upper three courses are pleasingly tapered and undercut at the lower join. The corners are beautifully finished and the whole has the necessary, bowed rise towards the centre. Under the east end, a chamber has been left between the bed-rock core and the inside of the steps. A similar situation is presented in the ruins of the Temple of Artemis below, where a cut in the rock drops down to a plastered cistern to either side.

· Along the ridge of Mount Smith behind—which takes its name from the redoubtable Admiral Sir William Sidney Smith (1764–1840) who lodged in a house on the hill in 1799 and 1800 during his campaigns against the French navy in the Napoleonic Wars—are the few scattered remains of what was the **acropolis** of Ancient Rhodes. At the highest point (111 m a.s.l.) to the northern end, were sited the two **temples of Zeus *Polieus* and of Athena *Polias*,** dominating the skyline from every direction of arrival by sea. Virtually nothing remains except for a few scattered column drums which mark the sites. To the east and a little below, however, extensive cutting of the living rock and stretches of walling give an intimation of the flight of terraces which led to them. These mark the edge of an interesting area of underground '*nymphaea*'.

· The several so-called *****Nymphaea** (or sanctuaries dedicated to the Nymphs) which sink deeply down from ground-level at the northern end of Mount Smith just east of the summit, probably began life as cisterns for collecting water from the several seeping springs in the area. A good way of understanding them is by beginning at the hidden hermitage or **grotto of Aghios Nikolaos** where the pagan cult of the nymphs seems to live on in a Christian guise (this lies just below the east side of Boreiou Ipeirou Street). Like the *nymphaea*, it originally housed a small seeping spring. Across the road from Aghios Nikolaos is a series of interconnected chambers with arched niches below ground level and rock-cut steps leading down into them. These are now completely uncovered, but may have been—at least partially—roofed: one of them (to the northeast) shows signs of a ledge for a roof. The complex is entered down a long rock-cut sloping '*dromos*' from the east. From ground level several openings are visible, but they interconnect and belong to the one complex. Further north, and just to the west (left) of the road is another complex conceived in the form of an atrium with a central *impluvium*, and apse-like areas to either end, with many rock-cut niches for votive objects above (especially on the north side). Some remains of carved decoration are visible: on the east side, a rock cut entablature and 'capitals' can still be seen. Below, cut steps are visible leading down into what must have been a pool of water whose level varied seasonally. Across the road (east side) is another grotto, more obviously designed as a cistern or well-house with access by steps. The springs which gave rise to this group of quasi-sanctuaries have dried now; but their importance to the inhabitants of the city is represented in the sacred spaces that they carved and created around the functional cisterns at their centre, and which they dedicated to the nymphs—protecting divinities of the springs.

THE ANCIENT CEMETERIES AND WALLS TO SOUTH AND SOUTHEAST

- **Ancient cemeteries** lay outside of inhabited areas. Rhodes was a large city with a wealthy population, and the area given over to burials therefore extends for nearly 3km to the south and southeast of the city. A lot of these can be seen by following the line of the main north/south artery of (Sophouli and) Tsaldari Streets (southeast of the acropolis hill). At the large junction with Ethnikis Antistasis is a small funerary area with some mosaic remains and small *oikia* for inhumation. By following Parthenopis Street west for 700m from this junction you come to the '**Monument of the Shield**'—a Hellenistic tomb, presumably of an important military figure given the monumental, emblematic carved shield over the door. The tomb extends in a long wall which must imitate the street façades of city houses of the period: to the right side the front is carved with the appearance of wooden doors. All this provided a quasi-theatrical backdrop to any ceremony of remembrance for the dead. The tomb was visible as it is today in the 19th century and was described by the British Antiquarian, Charles Newton. To the north of here is the area supposed by some archaeologists to be the site of the theatre of the ancient city.

- Further south on Tsaldari Street, at the junction with M. Petridi Street, is a large site where the meaning of a necropolis as a 'city of the dead' begins to make sense— arched galleries for sarcophagi (some *in situ*), with rectangular spaces for ossuaries above; steps to different levels and fragments of decorative and constructional elements in marble. An outcrop of natural rock above, with a large rectangular opening, serves as a rudimentary *propylon*: and to the southwest is the entrance to an impressive and spacious, **underground necropolis**, half hewn, half built. In the next cross street to the south (Ithakis Street) more superficial graves are being uncovered: and at other points, in the same area, are cave sepulchres and grave *loculi* with conches.

- Tsaldari Street ends where Konstantinou Ydreou Street cuts across it to the east (left): to the south of this street, the buildings end and you enter the northernmost extremity of Rhodini Park. Seven hundred metres of track southwest

through this part of the park brings you to the so-called
'**Tomb of the Ptolemies**' or '**Ptolemaion**'—an important,
probably 2nd century BC, Hellenistic funerary monument
with a pedimented doorway and **stuccoed façade**. This is
in effect an outcrop of natural rock fashioned into a 30m
square block. Its north side has been dressed with a row of
carved, engaged pilasters which have been plastered and
were once coloured, and which stand as if on a stepped
crepis. As with the 'Monument of the Shield', this may give
us a picture of how the street front of a well-to-do residence in Rhodes may have appeared. In the interior is a
transverse entrance chamber, leading into the main **burial
chamber** with niches for the deposition of bodies. Below
the façade are other, humbler burial *loculi* in the ground.
The whole block shows evidence of having been faced on
its other sides. The tomb's name has no historical foundation, and the ascription in local folklore to the ruling royal
family of Egypt with whom Rhodes had very close connections is no more than a reference to the fact that this is
one of the biggest tomb-complexes in the area. 100m to its
west is another complex of tombs, largely filled with earth,
but with fine carved cornices visible. A free-standing rock
in the field to the south has pediments and cornices carved
in it, holes and channels for drainage, and a rough cross
engraved in the top of the arch.

• The route out of the city to Aghia Marina and Kallithea down Kodringtonou [sic] Street (named after Admiral Sir Edward Codrington (1770–1851), hero of both the Battle of Trafalgar and of the Battle of Navarino (1827) in the Greek War of Independence), crosses the best preserved stretch of the **ancient city walls** which were re-built after the siege of Demetrios Poliorcetes in 304/303 BC. Areas of foundations of the walls and towers stretch to left and right. Beyond this point, the same street continues as Kallitheas Avenue and crosses the ditch of the walls on a bridge whose foundations and arches are those of a well-preserved **Late Hellenistic** or **Roman bridge** (1st century BC). Kallitheas Avenue passes first between the city's modern cemeteries, and then continues alongside the ancient cemeteries. The large area of the modern cemeteries between the road and the shore encompasses side by side an **Orthodox, Catholic, Jewish** and **Moslem Cemetery**—poignant testimony to the ethnic vicissitudes of the city's complex history. Across the avenue (west side) is a small **Allied War Graves** plot with burials of victims of the Second World War in the Dodecanese. On the west side of Kallitheas Avenue to the south are several more fine necropolises cut into the rock scarp. Decorated marble altars still stand in front of some of the sarcophagus chambers.

- Two kilometres along Lindou Avenue (the main road to Lindos which lies further to the west) out from the town centre, lies the entrance to **Rhodini Park**, to the right of the main road at the foot of a long hill. The park is a pleasant area of public gardens with dense shade, water, wandering peacocks and grazing deer. The fertile ravine was first laid out as a park in Ottoman times; but the site is often said to be that of the School of Rhetoric of Aeschines, the 4th century BC Athenian orator who went into voluntary exile in Rhodes some time after 330 BC. The glen is at one point traversed by an Ottoman aqueduct, adapted probably from a Roman predecessor. About 700m southwest from the entrance above the far side of the stream, a path leads up to the 'Tomb of the Ptolemies' (*see p. 154*).

THE NORTHWEST OF THE ISLAND AND KAMEIROS

From the aquarium at the northern extremity of the island, the coastal road to the southwest passes a number of disused windmills interspersed amongst the line of hotels on the waterfront: this stretch of coast is particularly exposed to the prevailing winds and was once the site of dozens of such mills. The road continues under the western slope of Mount Smith into the wide **bay of Trianda**, passing a curious line of identical, single-storey houses, with a small mosque and cemetery behind them. These were constructed in the late 1890s to accommodate an influx of Turkish refugees from Crete: the neighbourhood takes its name, *Kritiká*, from this. After 5km, a turning to the left leads in towards the hillside at **Malpasos**, whose name is linked with the legendary 'Dragon of Malpasso'. The monster dwelt in the gloomy, quarry-like gorge, full of fir and cypress, to the right under the rise of hill, and in the early 14th century it harassed the area seeking young maidens to devour.

THE DRAGON OF MALPASSO

So many knights had lost their lives trying to kill the monster of Malpasso that the Grand Master was obliged to forbid any to make further attempts on pain of expulsion from the Order. In spite of this proscription, one knight, Dieudonné de Gozon, matured a plan to tackle the dragon with the aid of two specially trained blood-hounds. His ruse, commemorated by Schiller in his ballad *Der Kampf mit dem Drachen*, was successful and the dragon was slain: but the Order's inexorable discipline required that the young knight was expelled and stripped of his habit. His appeal on the grounds of a motivation for the public good and safety was later accepted and Dieudonné stepped from legend into history to become the Order's Grand Master between 1346 and 1353. Such pieces of local history show how easily chivalric legends grew up around the court of the Knights of St John. They may even have been encouraged by them. Nonetheless, in order to quell any scepticism that might arise, the skull of the dragon was still to be seen as late as 1837, nailed to a post above the d'Amboise Gate.

TRIANDA

At the south end of the bay is the modern village of **Trianda** (7.5km). The centre is to the left of the main road where the low, stone church of **Aghios Nikolaos** (on Aghia Aikaterini Street, 200m west of the main square) is decorated with remnants of **wall-paintings** from the late 15th century. The legible scenes are few, but powerful. Some—in particular the **Mocking of Christ* on the north side of the vault, which constitutes a veritable glossary of rude gestures—are evoked by the artist with an originality, directness and vitality uncommon in Byzantine tradition. The back of the prothesis niche is also decorated with adoring angels and its borders edged with decorative designs.

Excavations near the coast at this point have uncovered an extensive and important **prehistoric settlement** established in the 16th century BC by the Minoans to facilitate trade between Crete and Asia. This was superseded by a larger Mycenaean settlement. At one of the lowest levels excavated, a 30cm layer of **volcanic ash** from Thera was found. At the moment of Thera's eruption in the 17th century BC, the prevailing wind in the Aegean was blowing from northwest to southeast, carrying the clouds of ash towards Rhodes and eastern Crete. Further back towards the base of the hill to the south, a wealth of burial finds have come to light from successive periods—Mycenaean through to Classical times. The finds are exhibited both in the Archaeological Museum of Rhodes and in the British Museum.

The village of Trianda occupies the site of the commercial area of **Ancient *Ialysos***, a prosperous independent Dorian city and one of the three major ancient settlements of the island, whose acropolis was on the summit of Mount Philerimos behind and to the south. It was famous in Antiquity for the *Diagóridai*, a family of oligarchs who also produced a number of Olympic victors: Diagóras, the most famous pugilist in antiquity, won the boxing competition no fewer than three times; three of his sons and two of his grandsons were also Olympic victors. He was celebrated by Pindar in his seventh *Olympian Ode*, of 464 BC: the ode, which tells the story of the island's identification with Helios, is an important source of Rhodian mythology. Tribute is still paid to Diagóras' fame: the new airport of Rhodes is also named after him.

PHILERIMOS AND THE ACROPOLIS OF *IALYSOS*

A winding road (signed) climbs up from Trianda through dense pine woods to the panoramic acropolis of ancient

Ialysos on the flat limestone summit of Mount Philerimos (267m). (*Open Apr–Oct 8.30–7.30; Nov–Mar 8.30–2.30; closed Mon.*) In spite of its importance in Antiquity, there is less for the modern visitor to see here than at either *Lindos* or *Kameiros*. A strange atmosphere prevails, due partly to the lifeless and over-restored mediaeval buildings which occupy much of the ancient sanctuary. On entering the enclosure, the remains of the 3rd century BC **Temple of Athena *Ialysia*** (which is probably built over the site of an earlier Phoenician temple) are visible directly in front of the monastery buildings. The stylobate is preserved, perfectly oriented to the cardinal points, and nearby are the drums of fluted columns, some of which retain vestiges of coloured stucco. In the 6th century AD an **Early Christian basilica** with three aisles was built over the temple. Its southern apse, just southeast of the temple, encloses a cruciform baptismal pool. Steps for immersion set in its floor are clearly visible, as well as remnants of its lining in Proconnesian marble. The existing church to the north is dedicated to the **Virgin of Philerimos** (or Filermo) and was heavily rebuilt by the Italians in 1931 to recreate the original mediaeval monastery which was mostly destroyed during the Turkish occupation. The plan is highly unusual, with three separate chapels inside, reached through a vaulted vestibule. To the left (south) is the Orthodox chapel, with a pleasing but slightly artless floor in polychrome marble; this was the first element of the complex to be built in the 13th century. To the right (north) of this, a further sanctuary and a subsidiary chapel were added by the Knights of St John in the 14th century to accommodate Roman Catholic rite. The Knights also added a bell-tower, of which the existing fortress-like version built by the Italians is no more than a fanciful memory.

THE ICON OF THE VIRGIN OF PHILERIMOS

The monastery's treasure was the priceless Icon of the Virgin of Philerimos, which was brought from Jerusalem in the 13th century and was believed to have been painted by St Luke. At times of great danger it was transferred to Rhodes to give the city divine protection. During the siege of 1522 it was lodged in the small church of St Mark (*see p. 43*) close to the bastion of St George. The icon was one of the only possessions the Knights took with them when they sailed away from Rhodes in January 1523. It was then kept in the Co-cathedral of St John in Valletta. Later, when Malta was surrendered to the French in 1798, the ill-starred Grand Master, Ferdnand von

Hompesch, sent the icon to Czar Paul of Russia; after the Bolshevik Revolution it was taken to Yugoslavia where it subsequently disappeared.

On the outside of the church (east side) is an unusually high pulpit in stone looking onto the monastery's tranquil cloister, lined with cells; beyond this is the former abbot's residence. The most unspoiled mediaeval survival is the tiny **chapel of St George 'Chostos'** ('underground'), below the level of the temple (*reached by turning left at the entrance to the site*) which was probably the crypt or funerary chapel of a church which once stood above. Its interior is covered in **wall paintings** which, though in poor condition, are still legible and of considerable interest: beneath some 17th century repainting are areas of the original 15th century images. In the vault, to the left are scenes of the *Passion of Christ*, and to the right, the *Early Life of the Virgin*; a dynamic *St George* occupies a large space towards the bottom of the east wall. On the side walls—painted as if to resemble figures on hanging tapestries—are kneeling knights being presented by their patron saints.

The hill-top to the east of the monastery bears the remains of much history: the commanding, wide panorama of the full sweep of the north of the island and the neighbouring islands and sea-routes explains why. At the northeast extremity are the remains of a Byzantine **fortress**, incorporating fragments of ancient building material; this fell to the Knights of St John in 1306, was enlarged by them and in turn was captured by Suleiman the Magnificent in 1522. From a camp on this vantage point the Sultan planned his siege of Rhodes. More recently the hill was contended by the Italians and Germans in 1943. Between the monastery and the castle on the promontory, are the steep entrances into two large underground **cisterns**, as well as a number of deep-cut water courses which traverse the area. The unexcavated foundations of ruined structures are everywhere on the plateau; erosion of its southern perimeter has left cisterns, staircases and habitations—the visible remains of the ancient city of *Ialysos*—hanging on the precipice. This was a large settlement, and densely inhabited in antiquity.

The treasure of the site (*currently closed*) is the ancient spring and the *****Doric, colonnaded water-fountain**, deep down the southern side of the acropolis amidst a stand of plane trees. Steps descend steeply for 50m, from the southern extremity of the archaeological enclosure, down to the elegant Hellenistic structure which dates from the mid 4th century BC and was reassembled in 1926 by Italian archaeologists. The colonnade is about 9m long, with the fountain tanks behind faced in marble with decorative lions' heads both on the rear wall, just above water level, and on the front: only one of these was perforated and functioned as a spout. One of the *antae* bears a scarcely legible inscription with regulations for the use of the fountain. The water, which rises close by, is particularly soft.

Outside the enclosure of Philerimos, from the small square beside the entrance, a tree-lined avenue leads west past relief images of the fourteen stations of the cross and culminates in a massive cement cross at the summit, which has the appearance of something constructed to withstand nuclear attack. To the left of the avenue, on the southern edge of the hill, are more ancient remains buried in the undergrowth; to the right are the ruins of a three-aisled cruciform church with narthex, dating from the 10th century. This was probably the *catholicon* and nucleus of another small monastic complex.

THE COASTAL VILLAGES, AND THEOLOGOS

Although considerably built up in the last few decades, the main coastal area southwest of Trianda still preserves a number of a beautiful neoclassical villas, some along the main road itself. Usually marked by venerable pine trees in their gardens (or in a couple of cases by immense *ficus magnoliae* trees), these elegant constructions date from a period of relative prosperity between 1890 and 1920. In general, the architecture of these villages has many surprises: in the central square of **Kremastí**, the next village after Trianda, a rusticated **Italianate gateway** and belfry in front of the church of the Panaghia Katholikí vies for attention with an attractive **library building** (1927) in the form of a small white temple which could have stepped straight from a rural town-square in the Mississippi delta; a tower, bizarrely decorated with ceramic and earthenware paraphernalia, can be glimpsed to the left on leaving the village to the south; and in Paradeísi, the next village to the southwest, a neoclassical school building bears the legend *Gymnaseio Paradeisíou*—'School of Paradise'. Kremastí is a lively centre, clustered around a small **castle** (just inland of the main road) whose base is a 15th century fortress built by the Knights and reworked in later epochs. The nearby church of **Aghios Nikolaos** has remains of 16th century wall-paintings in its interior: the church is entered through a broad and spacious, wooden-roofed porch in Turkish style. The village is noted for its nine-day **festival for the Assumption of the Virgin** (14–23 August) which combines religious ceremonies, athletic competitions, craft displays, music and dance, in a manner reminiscent of the ancient festivals of Antiquity.

At 13km a new road leaves to the left, connecting the airport with the east coast and the southern suburbs of Rhodes Town. Six kilometres down this road on the right, just south of the village of Pastida, is the Rhodes **Bee Museum** (*open Mon–Sat 8.30–3*) with a shop and interesting (live) apiary displays.

The coast road continues southwest past the airport. Opposite the terminal buildings on the east side of the main road is a small church with patches of 15th century wall-painting, figuring a regally dressed St Helen holding the True Cross. At 21km, the Hellenistic **Sanctuary of Erythimian Apollo** is signed to the left (500m). The epithet, *Erythimian*—'reddened' or 'flushed'—is unusual: but a widespread local tendency towards identification of Apollo with Helios may indicate that this is a dedication to Apollo as manifested in the incandescent colour of the setting or rising sun. Little remains to be seen of the temple: a succession of archaeologists' sounding trenches, partially revealing a crepidoma and some sanctuary buildings (constructed not in dressed marble, but in sandstone), with Early Christian overlay. Two sections of building-base(s) are recognisable (one to each side of the road) on a north-east/south-west orientation. A well

constructed ancient drain cuts east/west under the site.
This whole, low-lying area has yielded much archaeological interest: tombs from Mycenaean and Archaic periods,
and ancient architectural fragments from around the
church of Aghios Ioannis in the village of **Theologos**.

THE VALLEY OF THE BUTTERFLIES

Approximately 5km beyond the village of Theologos to
the south is **Petaloudes**, the 'Valley of the Butterflies'– too
renowned, perhaps, for the good of the insects themselves
(*access by admission fee, July–Sept 8.30–6; unrestricted and
free at other times of year*). This is a densely wooded valley,
coursed with streams and criss-crossed by wooden walk-
ways and bridges which aim to contain visitor access to
the remarkable spectacle of the large numbers of a single
species of colourful moth which congregate here during
the summer months.

PETALOUDES

These are not technically butterflies, but a kind of
moth which has habitually been drawn to this valley to mate in the summer by the number of storax
trees that grow here. The moth, first studied in the

Himalayas but later found on several continents, is a tiger-moth of the species *Callimorpha* (or *Euplagia*) *Quadripunctaria* (the second epithet referring to the pattern of the Roman numeral IV, visible on its upper right wing). They are generally referred to as 'Jersey tiger moths' in English. They come in large numbers from around the island and perhaps as far away as the Turkish coast to aestivate here, drawn by the humidity and the presence of the thin and smooth-limbed, *Styrax officinalis* and *Liquidambar orientalis* trees which line this valley and whose sweet smelling, golden-coloured resin—a principal ingredient of incense—attracts them. The moths are present and mating in greatest numbers from July to September, after which time they leave the area to lay their eggs elsewhere. The next generation will return again the following year to the valley. The grey-coloured moths rest with the head pointing downwards and their wings closed: but, if disturbed, they reveal the brilliant orange of their lower wings as they fly—often in considerable numbers—forming a silent, shimmering cloud of colour. Visitors anxious to see this display have for decades disturbed the creatures with clapping and noises, and this in turn has caused a marked decline in numbers. Some recent measures to control access (to the point even of a network of closed-circuit television cameras) as well as strenuous appeals for silence have helped to stem the decline to some extent. The endemic bellflower *Campanula rhodense* can also be seen in this area.

Less than 2km uphill, beyond the Petaloudes Valley, is the **monastery of Kalopetra**, built in 1784 by Alexander Ypsilantis, Prince of Walachia (modern-day southern Romania), who had been exiled by the Turkish authorities to Rhodes. The setting is peaceful with fine views.

Beyond the turning for Theologos the main coast road passes through Soroní. A turn to the south leads (3km) to the wooded rural monastery chapel and curative spring of **Aghios Syllas** or **Soulas** ('Saul'). The final chapter of Lawrence Durrell's *Reflections on Marine Venus* is dedicated to the extraordinary ritual, athletic, racing, eating, dancing and drinking celebrations that occur here on the saint's feast day (29–30 July), and which are a rich example of the continuity from pagan to modern in the rural Greek world.

ANCIENT *KAMEIROS*

At 35km, a turning in from the shore leads up through olives and pines, to the tranquil and beautiful site of *An-cient *Kameiros* or *Camirus* (*open Apr–Oct 8–7.30; Nov–Mar 8.30–2.30; closed Mon*).

General

In complete contrast to *Ialysos*, the site here is a clear and comprehensible unity, undisturbed by overbuilding in later epochs and remarkably well preserved by the in-filling dust (which Homer accurately describes as *arginóeis* ('chalky in colour'), *Iliad*, II, 656). Few other places in the Greek Islands give a more complete and un-fragmented picture of the layout of a small ancient centre than *Kameiros*. Every part of the site is visible from every other, and the simple and integral relationships between the areas can be easily understood: the civic and commercial area at the level of the entrance; the most important religious and administrative buildings at the crown of the hill; and the residential area—not banished to a suburb, but laid out between the two, in such a way as to give a sense of security to the inhabitants. One of the most interesting features of *Kameiros* is the city's system of storage and **distribution of water**, effected by a network of

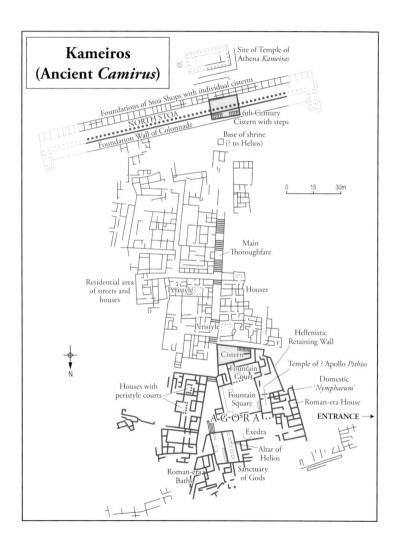

**Kameiros
(Ancient *Camirus*)**

Site of Temple of
Athena *Kameiras*

Foundations of Stoa Shops with individual cisterns

NORTH STOA

6th-Century
Cistern with steps

Foundation Wall of Colonnade

Base of shrine
(? to Helios)

0   15   30m

Main
Thoroughfare

Residential area
of streets and
houses

Peristyle

Houses

Peristyle

Hellenistic
Retaining Wall

Cistern

Fountain
Court

Temple of ? Apollo *Pithios*

N

Houses with
peristyle courts

Fountain
Square

Domestic
'*Nymphaeum*'

Roman-era House

A·G·O·R·A

ENTRANCE ➞

Exedra

Altar of
Helios

Roman-era
Baths

Sanctuary
of Gods

large underground conduits. The visitor today must imagine the sound of running and splashing water at many points throughout the ancient town.

Named after one of the grandsons of the nymph Rhode and Helios (Pindar, *Olympian* VII, 69–76), *Kameiros* was the smallest of the three original, Dorian settlements on the island. Its economy was primarily agricultural, and the need to store and transport its surplus produce of oil and wine was the stimulus for a vigorous, local ceramic industry. It possessed a shallow and rather exposed harbour—*Mylantia*—on the coast below: but it may also have used the more protected port, 13km further south along the coast at modern-day Kameiros Skala. This inconvenient state of affairs may have contributed to its willingness to participate in the creation of the new city of Rhodes in 407/8 BC, with its superb ports and commanding position for trade. *Kameiros* was devastated by an earthquake in 226 BC: this means that much of what is standing above ground dates from the rebuilding which followed that disaster.

The Site
Lower area
The visitor enters the site at the level of the commercial and civic centre, or *agorá*, of the city—a flat, open area artifi-

cially levelled, with a retaining wall below to the left, at the seaward extremity of the present enclosure. This space was bounded by a number of sacred buildings and by the fountain complex and public meeting-space to the south east side, against the central slope of the hill. To the right on entering is a **di-style temple**, oriented north/south, with two columns re-erected, probably dedicated to Pythian Apollo. Several different coloured materials have been used in its base to pleasing effect: a yellow threshold step on the front (south) side and a course of local marble at the lowest level of the base; originally this would have provided greater contrast since the upper areas of sandstone would have been rendered in white plaster. Inside, the base for the cult statue is visible, with a sunken treasury for offerings behind and two bases for votive objects to either side of the entrance of the *naos*. By the southwest corner of the temple is a large 3rd century BC **shrine** with a statue base in its interior. Further to the west, at the edge of the excavated area, are the remains of a **house of the Roman period** with an interior room with apse (possibly a small *nymphaeum*) still preserving some bright, coloured plaster.

The **Fountain Square** is the open rectangular area to your right: spacious and partially shaded, this would have been the busy social hub of the city. It is surrounded by the **bas-

es for votive statues in Lardos marble, many of them with beautifully clear inscriptions. A number have been moved by the archaeologists and lined up along the eastern edge of the area. On the north (seaward) side are two curiosities— densely inscribed stones of grey marble sculpted in a plastic and amorphous manner as if to simulate gnarled wood. The forms are too incomplete and the inscriptions too eroded to permit any certain identification of what these unusual items signified. The **fountain-house** proper lies to the south, with a row of erected columns in front (often inscribed on their sides) with incisions to hold in place cross-pieces from floor to waist level: some of these would have been of marble, but others of wood so as to permit entrance. A large trapezoid-shaped area of cisterns lay below the high, dressed-stone wall to the south behind: steps are cut descending this wall from top right. The water was contained by another wall directly behind the fountain courtyard or peristyle, with axial steps leading up to it from the colonnade and from the open square. This layout is seen most clearly from above. Note that the high, stone retaining walls mentioned above, as well as those along the east side of the area, have been largely reconstructed by the Italian archaeologists in the 1930s.

Leaving this area to the north (towards the sea), you pass through what was once a long enclosure wall with engaged columns. Beside it at a lower level are visible the bases of much earlier walls of the 5th century BC in '*poros*' limestone. At an angle, to the right, is an **exedra** with an altar or statue-base centrally placed in front: this was probably another, elegant votive dedication. Behind this is a terraced area referred to as the '**sanctuary of the gods**', containing parallel rows of altars to the various divinities whose names are inscribed on the front: '*Hestia*' (goddess of the hearth and home), '*Agathos Daimon*' (good fortune), etc. The long altar on the lower level was dedicated to Helios. Directly behind this sanctuary, in the northeast corner of the site, is the later **bath complex** with evidence of hypocaust and plastered walls for impermeability. From here the fine spectacle of the **stepped main street** opens out, rising uphill to the south with houses and shops to the left.

Middle area

The large **residential area**—still only partially excavated—is a pleasure to explore. The houses, as was typical of the Hellenistic period, were constructed around an open peristyle with a single, central entrance onto the street: the columns supporting the roof of the peristyle have been re-erected by the archaeologists in a couple of instances. The rooms off of the courtyards were small and the spaces between houses narrow. The walls would have been mostly plastered except at the external corners which are pleasingly finished in dressed stone-work: these corners were left un-plastered since they were more subject to knocks and damage. Some houses may have had wooden balconies. In all, the appearance might not have been that dissimilar from the old quarter of, say, Lindos today. A walk amongst the houses reveals stone water-jars and braziers in volcanic rock from Nisyros; fountain-bases in the centre of courtyard *impluvia*, paved with inlaid stones; niches for statues of divinities; cisterns, well-heads and small mill-stones for grinding. Everywhere underfoot are broken ceramic tiles (thick) and pots (thin)—even some red-glaze ware: stretches of stone water-conduits (Greek) and clay-piping (Roman) at ground level, are witness to the extensive water distribution system. Just before the steps begin, an iron grill covers the main street's drain which, though modified by the excavators, still possesses its original channel.

Upper area

At the top of the street the broad **acropolis area** opens out. To the left is a small rectangular shrine, standing apart and slightly off the axis of all the other buildings, though precisely oriented east/west. The first thing to locate at this level is the oldest element—a huge *Archaic cistern (6th century BC), carefully plastered and with two well-preserved flights of steps leading down into it. The capacity of this impressive construction is about 600 cubic metres of water. The duct leading water into it can be seen at the top of the eastern end of the south wall; the stone discs on the floor that look like column bases cover the exit holes, and could be moved in order to regulate the flow. The rim of the cistern is beautifully finished. It is generally supposed that this collected water from the roofs of the acropolis buildings; but its size, together with the extent of the network of conduits below, would point to there having formerly been some other and more constant source of water, which has now dried. It will be observed that the cistern is bisected by a foundation wall in yellow sandstone, constructed much later in Hellenistic times. This is because, after the earthquake of 226 BC, a **Hellenistic stoa** of remarkable dimensions (over 200m in length) was constructed to crown the whole width of the summit of the town. Such a *stoa* would consist of a colonnade in front, a wall of shop or office entrances set back under the colonnade, and a rear supporting wall. The front colonnade of this *stoa* was built up on the wall which bisects the cistern, and which extends further to east and west; the middle wall (i.e. the front wall of the shops/offices) runs just behind the cistern; and the base of the rear wall is visible below the line of trees behind, divided into room units. The floor of each one of these units is punctuated by a circular well-head or cistern cap. This row of large cisterns was what replaced the (by then) de-commissioned Archaic cistern. The coolness of this shady building with its wide north-facing panorama over the city and the surrounding islands must have made it an enviable place to gather, to do business, or simply to be cool and admire the view. The view in the opposite direction, to the south, is also magnificent; this would have been enjoyed by the sanctuary of the other great building which occupied this summit, the **Temple of Athena *Kameiras***. The visible remains here of a base and enclosure wall are from the last temple on the site, built after 226 BC to replace the earlier, classical Doric temple that had been shaken down. The vestigial remains of an altar and bothros (sacred pit) are visible beyond the east end, near to the south edge of the hill.

Much of the site is still to be uncovered. No theatre has yet been located, nor any substantial fortification walls. Cemeteries have been extensively explored on the lateral slopes, and the magnificent finds which they have yielded are in the Museum in Rhodes. Approximately 70m below the entrance to the site as you return towards the main coast road, a track to the right permits a good view of the lower wall-terracing and of an imposing **exedra**—possibly a *nymphaeum*.

SKALA KAMEIROU

The coastline to the immediate south of Kameiros is largely uninhabited. After 9 km is the village of **Madrikó**. A Myceneaean chamber tomb with *dromos* was found near here on the hill of Melissaki to the northeast: on a hillock further inland to the northeast are vestiges of Hellenistic and Roman habitation. At 51km (6km beyond Mandrikó) is the quiet harbour of **Skala Kameirou**, with two pleasant fish tavernas. The east side of the harbour has a long stretch of mediaeval walling, dating from an age when the port was in greater use. On the south escarpment, almost behind the 'Taverna Loukas', are the remains of a **Lycian tomb**. Most of its carved elements (pilasters etc.) have eroded, but the forms of the pediment and the architrave, cut in to the rock-face, are clear. The warm rock here seems particularly favoured by the 'Rhodes dragons', or *agama* lizards. These have more the appearance of iguanas (hence their name 'Rhodes dragons') and can grow to about 35cm in length: they are a principally African and west Asian species (*Agama stellio*). It is possible that they were brought to a number of the islands in the Aegean as part of the cult of Apollo with whom they are associated.

From the harbour at Skala Kameirou the F/B *Nikos Express* leaves for Chalki every day at 14.30 throughout the year.

THE NORTHEAST OF THE ISLAND

KOSKINOU, KALLITHEA AND FALIRAKI

The east coast of the island to the south of Rhodes is sheltered from the prevailing winds, punctuated by majestic headlands and has an altogether more intimate feel than the flatter shore-line of the west coast. The greatest concentration of tourist infrastructure and large hotels is to be found here.

From the Hellenistic bridge (*see p. 155*) at the southern end of Kodringtonou Street (*0km point for distances given*), Kalitheas Avenue leads south out of the city between the main modern cemetery and the area of the ancient necropolises. There are substantial visible remains of the latter to the right of the road, with altars, sarcophagi and rock-cut burial chambers dating from the 2nd century BC through to the 2nd century AD. After 4km, **Koskinou** is visible on the top of the escarpment to the right. This is a largely residential area which has preserved many attractively coloured houses in both neoclassical and traditional architecture of the 19th century.

At **Kallithéa** (7km), **thermal springs** rise close to the shore: these were known in Antiquity and their therapeutic qualities allegedly recognised by Hippocrates. Their average temperature is only 19°C and the water is indicated for drinking more than for bathing. The ***buildings of the thermal spa** designed by Pietro Lombardi in 1927 add magic to an otherwise ordinary stretch of coast. In the way in which they sympathetically relate to the landscape and create pleasing, semi-covered spaces that are neither inside nor outside, they represent what is best and most imaginative in Italian colonial architecture in the Dodecanese.

The Italian occupying forces landed here in May 1912. The decision to consecrate the spot with a grandiose spa was aimed principally at encouraging holidaymakers to the island. Lombardi created an unusual complex of low circular buildings and radiating hemicycles which combines many references, both local and foreign; there are memories of the Gothic portals (e.g. Aghia Paraskevi) of the Knights, the open stoas of Ancient Greece, and the *chochlakia*, pebble pavements of the Dodecanese, mixed with orientalising, quasi-Moorish touches and embellished with palms. Once again, the key-note form is the unusually wide and low arch, springing from short quarter-columns, whose effect is greatly to accentuate breadth and lateral space. After the War, the bath complex was abandoned to an increasingly romantic state of decay. In 2003 a project for their complete restoration was begun by the Greek authorities, aimed at opening the complex commercially to the public once again: this has certainly reversed the decay of the structures, but at the same time has swept away much of their once elegiac appeal.

After Kallithea the road descends into the long bay of **Faliráki**—the often strident tourist epicentre of the island. Below the headland at the far southern end of the bay is the church of **Prophitis Amos**, a 17th century single-aisle church with pebble floor and vestiges of its original paintings on the walls and on the masonry templon screen.

AFANDOU AND THE PSINTHOS AREA

At 16 km, the bay of Afándou opens out, with indications (left) to the island's golf course (a rarity in the Greek Islands). Half-way along the bay, and midway between the main road and the parallel road along the shore-line, is the interesting church of the **Panaghia Katholikí**. The tiny, cruciform, 16th century church is huddled into the remains of an Early Christian basilica whose *opus alexandrinum* floor in polychrome marble can still be seen outside the west door. Just to the left of the door is a clerical **throne**, constructed from heterogeneous marble elements taken from the early church. On the north exterior, some of the masonry and two Rhodian marble columns from the Early Christian basilica are embedded in the wall of the church, and other remains of Early Christian buildings can be seen further to the east. Inside, the floor is pebbled and the walls are covered with lively but damaged **paintings**. On the south wall, above a row of tormented figures in hell (predominantly female), bound by serpents and licked by flames, is the figure of St Michael dispensing justice; to the left of him are several interesting 18th century **votive graffiti of sailing ships**, scratched into the plaster by grateful sailors.

Eight and a half kilometres inland of Afándou is the quiet and undisturbed rural centre of Psinthos: in its vicinity are two early churches—delightful for their simplicity, antiquity and setting; both are reached by taking the road to the left (signed to Archipolis) on entering the village, which passes the springs of Fasólou. Less than 2km from the junction and just to the left of the road is the minuscule 13th century church of **Moni Aghia Triada** (*key on nail to left of door*). The **wall-paintings**, which cover every surface, are possibly contemporaneous with the building though they are now much obscured by candle soot and have repainted faces in places; on the south wall is a *Deësis* with a finely painted St John the Baptist. On the west wall to the left of the door, the donor, between two rose-trees, presents the church to the Saviour. Further down the same road is the **church of the Panaghia Parmeniótissa** (*reached by turning left at the only eucalyptus tree after 2km—600m of asphalt and 1.4km of track; the church is hidden from view on a small rise about 100m from the road*). This is another tiny, isolated building in un-rendered stone. Although the 15th century **paintings** are generally not in good condition, one area in the apse (above and to the right) shows the careful quality of the draughtsmanship. There are scenes of the *Life and Passion of Christ*, and a fine *Saint Cosmas* on the south wall.

KOLYMBIA, EPTA PIGHES ('SEVEN SPRINGS') AND TSAMBIKAS

At the south end of Afándou Bay is the settlement of **Kolymbía**. Originally named 'San Benedetto', it was created as a model agricultural village by the Italians in the 1930s for settling colonists. Its grid-plan of streets and its style of architecture are similar to many of the settlements of the Pontine Marshes, south of Rome, created by the political regime in Italy at about the same time and with similar aim. Inland of Kolymbía a turning (right) off the main road (at 22km), leads west up a shallow valley to **Eptá Pighés** (3km) where, in a ravine of pines and plane trees, the confluence of seven, year-round springs feeds a small lake used for irrigation. The place is a peaceful retreat from the heat in summer, and is frequented by picnickers and peacocks. Among the trees found here are a variety of arbutus, Valonia oaks, Oriental planes, azaroles and some storax trees, recognisable in spring by their mass of white flowers.

After the Epta Pighes junction, the road rises with Mount Tsambíka to the left; at 23.5km, a turning to the left leads up to the **hermitage of Panaghia Tsambíka Kyrá** on its panoramic summit. After the road finishes its steep climb, a further 300 steps lead through cedar trees to the 16th century chapel on the summit (287m a.s.l.). The foundation is related to the appearance of a miraculous icon on the hill, and in all probability replaces an earlier pagan cult of Artemis in the same place. The Virgin of Tsambika is especially the protectress of women in pregnancy, and of problems related to conceiving and bearing children—matters which came also into the purview of Artemis in antiquity. Inside the chapel, the whitewash has been spared at one point to reveal the fine, bearded head of a saint, in style contemporary with the foundation: to the south is a small hermit's cell. The views are magnificent. In the valley below and beside the main road (2 km further to the south) is the **monastery of the Panaghia**

Tsambika (1760), a spacious grouping of buildings, shaded by an ilex tree of truly remarkable size.

ARCHANGELOS

Archángelos (28km) is the principal settlement between Rhodes and Lindos—deliberately hidden from view from the sea by an escarpment, so as to avoid the unwanted attentions of coastal pirates, and dedicated to the Archangel Michael for yet further protection. The area is rich in a light clay ideal for pots, and for this reason it had a flourishing **ceramic production** from as far back as the 5th century BC: later, high quality bricks were also produced here. The anonymous account of the building of Santa Sophia in Constantinople known as the *Narratio* alleges that the bricks in its dome were made in Rhodes, and that 12 of them would weigh only as much as one ordinary brick: these would have been Archangelos bricks. The town today has a number of traditional and decorated houses. The **castle**, built by the Knights of St John in the mid-15th century, dominates the horizon. It is best approached by foot through the town from where the beautiful, abstract contours of the masses of rock rising up against the well-preserved curtain of walls can best be appreciated. Though impressive from below, the castle is small, occupying a tight triangular space with a modern chapel and the remains of only a couple of inner buildings at floor level inside the enceinte: it must have functioned more as a look-out and signalling station than as a long-term defensive refuge. High on the west wall, in a carved stone frame, are the coats of arms of Grand Masters Zacosta (1461–67) and Orsini (1467–76), executed in grey marble from Lardos.

One kilometre after rejoining the main Lindos road south from Archangelos, on the left is the whitewashed church (recently re-roofed and set in a walled enclosure) of the twin saints, **Aghii Theodori** (1377) whose interior is entirely covered in 14th/15th century **paintings**. In a niche in the north wall, the two Theodori are seen on horse-back in mirror poses against a blue firmament, while the Almighty presides from above.

PHERAKLOS CASTLE

After Archangelos the road descends into a wide coastal plain. At the foot of the descent (33km) a turning is indicated to the right towards **Pheraklos Castle**, visible 2km to the south of the road. From its size and magnificence it is clear that this castle, unlike the fort at Archangelos, was a protective refuge for the local population in times of danger and was designed to endure a siege: the large **cisterns** inside confirm as much—some so deep that it is hard to imagine they could ever have been filled completely. When the Knights arrived in Rhodes in 1306, a Byzantine castle which they proceeded to capture already existed here; they appear entirely to have rebuilt it for themselves over the next two decades, maintaining the same foundations but reconstructing the walls and cisterns. The masonry does not use the limestone of the immediate area but rather a 'poros' stone transported from further south on the island. It is fixed with extensive use of brick tiles, potsherds and mortar in the interior of the walls. After settling in Rhodes, the Knights often used the castle as a detention centre for prisoners and errant members of the Order. The enceinte is entered on the southwest side: nearby, the base of a look-out tower is visible at the highest point. The most impressive remains on the summit are the variety of deep cisterns—some vaulted, others cylindrical and originally domed. A number of deep galleries were cut into the rock of the hill at ground level for refuge and storage during the Second World War; the entrance to one of these is on the right of the path as you descend.

At 42km the main road divides, the right-hand branch continuing to the south of the island (*see Southern Rhodes*). The left branch leads after 3.5km to Lindos.

LINDOS

Lindos has the most impressive archaeological remains, the oldest Byzantine churches, and the finest vernacular buildings on the island: it is a town of architectural beauty in a consummate natural setting. This inevitably means that the flood of visitors in its tiny streets and spaces, from Easter to October, is daunting: on days when large cruise-ships are in the port of Rhodes the problem can take on impossible proportions. For a peaceful visit it is wise to go as early in the morning or as late in the afternoon as can be reconciled with the opening times of the acropolis (*see below*). The light and shadow are at their best at these times and further enhance the natural beauty of the setting.

From a distance—whether approaching by sea or by land—the reason for the founding and for the enduring importance of Lindos is clear: an isolated and panoramic natural rock acropolis and two splendid bays for ports. In addition, there is a plentiful spring. These three elements compensated for a terrain which offered little possibility of agriculture and meant that Ancient *Lindos*, unlike *Ialysos* and *Kameiros*, had to live primarily on trade. Of the three ancient Dorian cities it was always the most important and maintained its influence, especially as a religious centre, long after the 5th century BC *synoecism* and the creation of the federal state of Rhodes. Lindos acquired prestige also through her early colonies, in particular *Gela* in Sicily and *Phaselis* in Lycia on the south coast of Asia Minor. The Lindians excelled in navigation and maritime commerce, developing a code of law for shipping on which 'Rhodian (Maritime) Law' was later based: this in turn became the basis for Roman, and latterly modern, Maritime Law.

Neolithic and Mycenaean occupation of the promontory are attested by archaeology, while the cult of Athena *Lindia* appears to go back at least to the 10th century BC. Most of what the visitor sees today, however, dates from a later re-building during the 4th century BC. The site was too important to neglect in later epochs; passing crusaders and expanding Venetian trade brought Lindos prosperity in the 12th century, further nurtured by the Knights of St John who expanded the Byzantine presence, fortified the acropolis and stationed a permanent garrison here. The prosperity of many of the families of Lindos is reflected both in the dignified and decorated mansions which are to be found in the narrow streets of the lower town and in the finely painted churches.

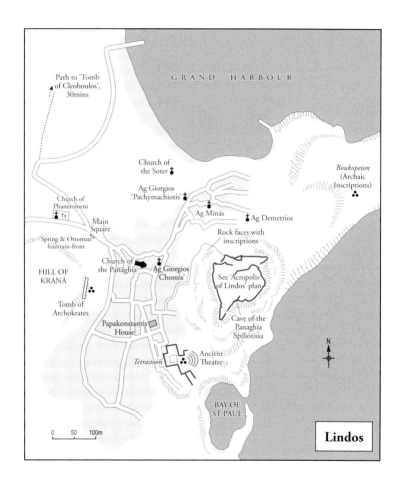

Path to 'Tomb
of Cleoboulos',
30mins

GRAND HARBOUR

Church of
the Soter

Ag Giorgios
'Pachymachiotis'

Ag Minás

Ag Demetrios

Boukopeion
(Archaic
Inscriptions)

Church of
Phaneromeni

Main
Square

Spring & Ottoman
fountain-front

Church of
the Panaghia

Ag Giorgios
'Chostós'

Rock faces with
inscriptions

See 'Acropolis
of Lindos' plan

HILL OF
KRANÁ

Tomb of
Archokrates

Cave of the
Panaghia
Spiliótissa

Papakonstantis
House

Tetrastoön

Ancient
Theatre

N

BAY OF
ST PAUL

0   50   100m

Lindos

THE LOWER TOWN

From the main junction above the town, the road descends steeply past the **cemetery** and the chapel of the **Phaneroméni** on the left to a *plateia* shaded with mulberry trees: to one side is the town's ancient water-source of soft spring-water, flowing out from an 18th century **marble front** with partially abraded inscription in Osmanli script. Opposite is a bust of Ioannis Zigdis, a distinguished politician and economist of the last century from Lindos.

The church of the Panaghia

On entering the town, the low form of the **church of the Panaghia**, marked by an ornate bell-tower in local 'poros' limestone, is visible almost immediately on the left. The present church, of Latin-cross form with octagonal drum and cupola, was restored and enlarged in 1489 by the Grand Master Pierre d'Aubusson, whose coat of arms is clearly visible above the entrance to the church: the original foundation is much earlier, possibly 12th century. An **ancient altar** is immured into the upper south wall, and two further altars have been reused as benches for seating, to left and right of the west door. The low and broad interior of the church is one of the most completely and homogeneously **decorated interiors** in the Dodecanese. The floor is a fine example of *chochlakia* work (black and white pebble inlay), providing both tactile and aesthetic pleasure. The complete programme of **paintings** (restored in 1927) which cover all the interior walls is by Gregory of Symi, signed and dated 1779 in an inscription on the lintel in the north transept. The wooden **iconostasis** and bishop's **throne** are of 1620 by Ignatius of Lesbos. The disposition of the paintings throughout the church follows the classic iconographic topography for a building of this form: the *Pantocrator* in the dome; the four *Evangelists* in the pendentives; scenes from the *Life of Christ* in the upper nave; interceding *Saints* below at shoulder level to the congregation; and the ***Last Judgement*** (in this church, particularly worthy of note) over the west door—to be seen by the faithful as they leave for the evil of the world outside. The pictures lack some of the mystical grace of early Byzantine painting: by the 18th century, Greek painters were beginning to feel the influence of the more literal and narrative traditions of Western painting. This clarity of conception does however mean that the biblical scenes are easily identifiable. Only the lower register on the sides of the main nave bears scenes which are less familiar, because they represent the 24 stanzas of the Acathist Hymn in praise of the Mother of God. Visiting the **Church Museum** (*open daily Apr–Oct*), gives the possibility of seeing the finest and earliest wall-paintings of the complex, over the outside door of the funerary chapel of the north transept. According to the inscription, these date from 1674. A beautiful image of the ***Virgin '*Hodeghetria*'** (of 'Guidance') centred over the door, is framed by a standing priest (right), and a remarkable scene of the *__Righteous Man's Death__** (left), in which the dying man, lying down and draped in a blanket, receives the Eucharist from an angel while David (crowned) plays a dirge on a viol accompanied by other angels with various, stringed, musical instruments. The whole scene is of a work of high quality. Below is a more damaged scene of the *Sacrifice of Isaac*. The museum itself contains a fine embroidered *epitaphios* and a small collection of liturgical objects: in the open-air courtyard, are fragments of a classical frieze.

Of particular interest in the streets of the old town are a number of small and venerable **Byzantine churches**; and many fine **Patrician mansions** in a unique vernacular architecture. A brief overview of these two groups follows.

The early Byzantine churches

Lindos has a number of small Byzantine churches which substantially predate the arrival of the Knights on the island. Several of them have the remains of wall-paintings which range in date from the 12th to the 15th centuries, but whose condition is generally not good. Two of the churches—Aghios Giorgios Chostós and Aghios Giorgios Pachymachiótis—are dedicated to the same saint, but possess different epithets: '*chostos*', 'on or in a mound of earth', is often attached to semi-underground churches or chapels in low-lying hollows, while '*pachymachiotis*' refers to the saint as 'thickly armed for battle'. **Aghios Giorgios Chostós** (pre-11th century) is the oldest of the group: it sits in a declivity just below the northeast corner of the main square at the edge of the town. Its domed, inscribed-cross plan presents a compact, almost cuboid exterior with cylindrical drum. Inside there are several layers of superimposed wall-paintings from different epochs: the figures of the patriarchs and saints in the apse are late 12th century, while the unusual non-figurative design of crosses and medallions may be a century earlier. **Aghios Giorgios Pachymachiótis** is reached by taking the path that descends round the west and north sides of the church of the Panaghia. It too has an inscribed-cross design, with dome. Inside it bears an inscription on the southern side of the apse dating the building and its decoration to 1394/5. Above it is the tiny, 12th century church of **Aghios Minás**: the scene of the *Ascension* on the sanctuary vault is contemporaneous with the church's construction, while most of the other paintings are 15th century. The barrel vaulted church of **Aghios Demetrios**, higher up and at the end of the town to the northeast has faded 15th century painting on its north wall. From this side of the town the attractive form of the late 13th century **church of the Soter** ('Saviour') is visible far below, a short distance behind the beach on the north side of the town within a walled enclosure. It appears to be built across ancient walls in one corner: some Early Christian fragments lie in the vicinity.

The mansions of Lindos

In the labyrinth of the town's narrow streets are many well-preserved private houses—examples of a fine local architectural style which emerged in the 16th century. The **Papakostantis House** of 1626 (now a café) is the most accessible example and is also a pleasant place for refreshment. Stone-built, flat-roofed, and generally constructed around two or three sides of a flowering courtyard which is densely paved with the characteristic black and white pebble floor in abstract designs or figuring cypress trees or ships, the houses nearly always present a **monumental doorway** to the street outside: this is characteristically embellished with a striking stone door-frame, often

carved in a 'rope' design and surmounted with a decorated lintel or arch figuring doves, flowers, rosettes or
crosses, and sometimes bearing the date and family name
of the owners. Windows, occasionally with ogival frames,
may be similarly decorated. A peculiarity of some of the
houses is a windowed room on the upper floor built out
across the street from one side to the other, which affords
views of the street and its life. Most of the houses are built
over a cistern cut into the rock below the courtyard pavement. Inside, the main reception area generally faces the
entrance across the courtyard while the service rooms are
to the side(s). Decorated wooden ceilings (see, in particular, the **Ioannis Krikis House**, of 1700) were supported
by a single, wide, pointed arch: the furniture was heavily
carved, and the floor often paved with intricate designs.
Fine coloured ceramics adorn the walls: these are mostly
examples of—or pieces inspired by—17th century Iznik
ceramic work from Ottoman Turkey. Later on, this kind
of ceramic-work was exported through Lindos, and subsequently imitated locally in workshops in the town. It
became known abroad as '**Lindos ware**'.

THE UPPER TOWN—ACROPOLIS

(*Open Apr–Oct 8–7.30; Nov–Mar 8.30–2.30; closed Mon only in winter.*)

The inhabited settlement was never contiguous with the acropolis, but separated by a clear break of open rock and pine-trees. Visible to the right before reaching the entrance gate to the acropolis, are ancient **votive inscriptions** to the gods cut into the facets of the rock outcrops beside the pathway. (*A couple—one particularly long—may be seen clearly from the path as you climb up, at about shoulder height and higher, on the outcrop of naturally faceted rock to the right-hand side, just as the path turns right into the last straight stretch up to the entrance.*) Once through the outer gate, there is a shaded terrace punctuated by three prominent mouths of large, plaster-lined **Byzantine cisterns**: the acropolis had no spring within its walls, and depended on water collected in such cisterns; there are many more above, on the summit.

At the first turn in the path the visitor is faced with an impressive *****votive relief of the stern of a ship**, and to its left a **dedicatory exedra**—both skillfully carved into the living rock. Though contiguous, these are two separate dedications. An **inscription** on the side of the

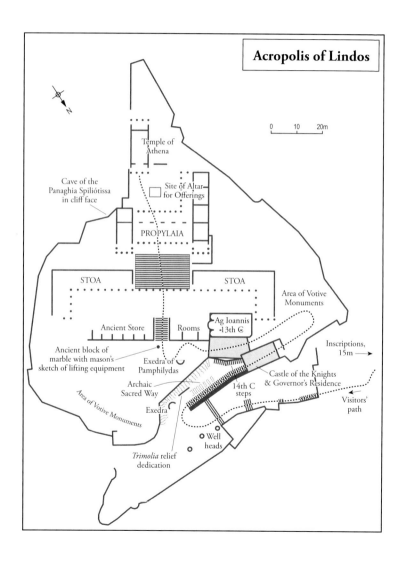

Acropolis of Lindos

N

0   10   20m

Temple of
Athena

Cave of the
Panaghia Spiliótissa
in cliff face

Site of Altar
for Offerings

PROPYLAIA

STOA   STOA

Area of Votive
Monuments

Ancient Store   Rooms   Ag Ioannis
-13th C

Inscriptions,
15m →

Ancient block of
marble with mason's
sketch of lifting equipment

Exedra of
Pamphilydas

Castle of the Knights
& Governor's Residence

Archaic
Sacred Way

14th C
steps

Visitors'
path

Area of Votive Monuments

Exedra

Well
heads

Trimolia relief
dedication

ship states that the work was 'dedicated to Agesander, son of Mikion, by the people of Lindos', and that it was the work of the Rhodian sculptor, Pythocritus of the 3rd/2nd centuries BC. Delicate chisel and point work can still be seen on the surface. Stylistic similarities have linked the piece and its artist to the *Winged Victory of Samothrace* in the Louvre. The kind of ship meticulously portrayed here possessed two rudders or steering paddles: visible are the helmsman's station on the near side, and a part of the serpentine shape of the rudder holding (something similar can be seen on a Venetian gondola). A break in the carving shows where a sculpted rudder itself would have projected downwards—if not in stone, perhaps added in wood. The boat's deck acted as the base for a statue of Agesander, possibly wearing the golden crown referred to in the inscription below. The **exedra** to the left may be a little earlier; it surrounds a base on which an honorific statue would have stood. Much later, in the 3rd century AD, the long inscription (originally picked out in red) was added by Aglochartos, priest of Athena *Lindia*.

To the left of the present stairs leading up to the acropolis there are vestiges of the **ancient Sacred Way** and steps. Much higher up to the left, is a flight of 14th century steps added by the Knights of St John, which originally gave access directly into the **Governor's Residence** by means of a wooden drawbridge. The Residence—now extensively restored—dates from the period of Grand Master Pierre d'Aubusson (1476–1503) and bears his arms in grey Lardos marble high up on the exterior wall: its interior was once painted with garlands, landscapes and coats of arms. These have faded considerably, and some areas have been removed to safety in Rhodes; the building now houses the local archaeological offices. The security of the building relies—as does the whole enceinte of walls—on the natural defences of the steep site, rather than on any ingenious military architecture. Some substantial machicolations can be seen high above the main door however.

The vaulted entrance, containing a number of capitals and finely inscribed altars and statue bases, gives onto an inner esplanade covered with many more of the same. This (only a fraction of the total number on the site) gives some indication of the forest of **votive statuary** in bronze and marble, as well as paintings and other works of art, which would have greeted the pilgrim in ancient times: in addition to the mute evidence of these fragments, writers (Philostratos, Plutarch and Pliny) also mention the works of art and spoils of war which were dedicated here—each piece vying for attention with the next.

The platcau of the acropolis is a roughly triangular area of 8,400sq. m rising to a height of 116m. The layout we see today dates from a building program begun in the 4th century BC; before that the **Archaic Sacred Way** had led across the open area, from the entrance directly up to the Temple of Athena at the summit. Some part of its paving can be seen in the floor, beside the long base of a Hellenistic monument, in the undercroft beneath the Governor's Residence reached by turning sharply to the left. This passage in turn leads out onto another esplanade crowded with more fragments of broken monuments. To the right, a line of (restored) **vaulted chambers**, originally built in the 1st century BC and used as storage spaces, support the first terrace of the grand approach to the Temple of Athena, created during the Hellenistic re-building. Just in front of the foot of the staircase that divides this line of vaults, is a rare and pleasing curiosity—a block of stone on the ground which fortuitously preserves an **ancient mason's sketch** of a piece of lifting machinery, scratched into the surface facing away from the steps.

To the left is a dark grey **marble exedra** which—according to the inscription at its back—was surmounted in the 3rd century BC by a bronze statue of Pamphilydas, priest of Athena. At the northern (left) extremity of the area once stood a Roman pro-style temple (no longer visible), which faced towards the Temple of Athena. The wide area in front, littered with ancient material, shows how four different colours of stone have been used on the acropolis:

- *Lardos marble*; an indigenous, mottled-grey marble quarried a few miles to the west of Lindos, sometimes tending to a solid, dark grey, used especially for inscribed surfaces;
- *Cycladic marble* (from Paros/Naxos); small amounts of this have been used, mainly for sculptural needs or decorative refinement;
- a homogeneous, deep rust-red '*poros*' limestone from the area of Atávyros;
- the honey-coloured '*poros*' limestone of the native rock of the acropolis.

The Temple and its approach

The **grand ascent** up to the temple at the summit is very much an expression of the Hellenistic mind—symmetrical, cadenced, theatrical, and with a grandiose and rather impersonal sense of ceremony about it. Note how, although this approach is symmetrical within itself, the reason for its existence—the Temple of Athena—steadfastly refuses to be included in its axis and remains to one side, clinging to its historic site. There are **three phases of building** in the whole complex, which all followed on from the restoration of the temple itself after its destruction by fire in 392 BC: 1. the *propylaia* enclosing the temple's sanctuary at the top, which date from shortly after the fire, i.e. the early 4th century; 2. the wide stoa on the next level down which dates from 300–290 BC; and 3. the terrace and vaulted storage areas below the stoa, which were the last elements to be added, around 100 BC.

As well as mentally preparing and physically corralling pilgrims for the approach to the temple, the **wide *stoa*** served as a shaded space where votive gifts—especially paintings—could be exhibited. It has been minimally reconstructed at the beginning of the last century to give at least some idea of its form. Originally, the Doric colonnade would have run the entire width of the building (87m); but its roof was omitted in the centre to allow a clear view of the next flight of steps up to the main ***propylaia***. These—only visible in foundations now—were in effect two contiguous *propylaia*: one symmetrical Doric colonnade at the top of the flight of stairs with two slightly projecting wings at either end; and an internal colonnade which was L-shaped, and which gave on to the temple. They marked the boundary of the sanctuary; access beyond this point was limited and the area could be entered only after ritual purification.

The **Temple of Athena** itself seems small after such a grand approach: it measures only 22m x 8m and is am-

phi-prostyle, tetrastyle in design, i.e. possessing a projecting four-column portico at either end. It hugs the very
edge of the southern precipice: its placing, its size and its
form, all faithful to the older Archaic temple that stood
here until the fire of 392 BC, traces of whose **crepidoma**
can be seen in the bed-rock of dark limestone inside the
present building. There has been considerable restoration, but much of the west wall is original; the east wall
rises straight from—and seems to grow out of—the rock
of the precipice. The stone would originally have been
covered with a layer of light-coloured plaster.

The temple has a long history: according to Herodotus (*Histories* II.182) it was the Danaids in their flight from the sons
of Aegyptus who established the cult; according to Diodorus
(5.58.1) it was Danaus himself. One of the temple's early
donors, the pharaoh Amasis, dedicated here a remarkable
linen corselet. In 392 BC fire destroyed the temple and a great
many of its dedications. When it was rebuilt, the worship of
Zeus *Polieus* was added and, at the same time, Athena became identified as Athena '*Polias*'. The original archaic cult
statue inside the temple was probably a wooden image of the
goddess, seated and wearing a golden diadem. It would have
been protected by a railing. Such was the fame and influence of the statue of *Athena Parthenos* by Pheidias in Athens,

however, that this original seated Athena was replaced in the 5th or 4th century by an image of the goddess, standing and armed—as in the Parthenon. It must have been this statue that was transported to Byzantium by Theodosius in the 5th century AD when the temple cult was officially suppressed and which apparently perished in a fire there later that century.

The entrance to the temple was at the north: on either side of it were two inscribed plaques in grey Lardos marble with the **chronological lists of the priests of Athena *Lindia* (*see box below*)**, running from 406 BC through to 47 AD. These precious records were removed in the Middle Ages and used as floor slabs in the church of Aghios Stephanos, only to come to the world's attention again when the church was removed and the area excavated in early 1900s: they are rare historical documents of great value.

In the narrow area in front of the south entrance are signs of extensive Archaic cutting in the bedrock. The view from the edge down to the perfectly formed natural harbour below, where tradition holds that St Paul took refuge from a storm, is unforgettable.

The pathway back to the exit, which descends by steps to the west, passes by a deep water-storage pool—part natural, part cut into the bed-rock—and continues to-

wards the massive supporting wall for the terrace of the
western end of the *stoa*—its regular, rectangular stone
blocks, elaborately rusticated in customary Hellenistic
fashion. Above it and to the north are the tall ruins of
the three apses of the east end of the 13th century, Byzantine **church of Aghios Ioannis**. Its rounded windows
and arches are a marked contrast to so much ancient rec-
tilinearity.

Other ancient remains outside the Acropolis, and the Tomb of Cleoboulos.

Around the base of the Acropolis hill are three further
important ancient sites. Below the southwest side, and
reached by taking a right-hand (south) route through the
lower town from the church of the Panaghia, is the **ancient theatre** (4th century BC), whose *cavea* of seats is cut
into the living rock of the slope. Although only the central part is still visible today, its design is clear with a deep
diazoma separating the lower nineteen rows of seats from
the upper seven. It would have had a capacity of almost
2,000 spectators. A cut in the centre of the *diazoma* suggests that the customary shrine to Dionysos, divinity of
the spirit of drama, was placed here. Opposite the *cavea*,
and across the *orchestra*, the position of the original *proscenium* is marked by cuttings in the rock.

Almost contiguous with the *proscenium* of the theatre are the remaining foundations of a large, almost square, building with peristyle which was constructed over a century later than the theatre. This cloister-like building is referred to as the **Tetrastoön**; its exact function is unknown. The fact that no fewer than three churches had been built on the site in later times, and that a number of Christian burials were found here, would suggest that it was used for cultic purposes in antiquity, since it was always the habit of early Christian communities to transform places of pagan worship into churches or sacred Christian sites. It was here, in the floor of the now demolished church of Aghios Stephanos, that the inscribed stones with the **lists of Athena's priests** were found, as well as the '**Lindian Chronicle**'.

THE LINDIAN CHRONICLE

In 99 BC the people of Lindos commissioned an inscription recording the dedications that had been made in their temple to Athena since its foundation. Two men were selected and instructed to 'inscribe from the letters and public records and from any other evidence, whatever might be fitting regarding the offerings and the visible presence of the goddess'.

First published by the Danish archaeologist, Christian Blinkenberg in 1912, it is known as the '*Lindian Chronicle*', and is one of the longest inscriptions to have survived from the Hellenistic Greek world. It is now in the Archaeological Museum in Copenhagen. The chronicle gives the name of the dedicator, lists the objects dedicated (with a description of the material from which they were made and any inscription they might possess) and finally gives the 'sources' that named and described any objects that no longer existed. The dedications include gold, jewellery, weaponry, statuary (e.g. a 'cow and calf fashioned in wood', a 'wooden Gorgon with marble head', etc.). Amongst those who made the dedications, are mentioned Cleoboulos, Artaphernes (brother and general of the Persian king, Darius), Alexander the Great, Ptolemy I of Egypt, and Pyrrhus, king of Epirus. A fascinating final section of the inscription narrates three miraculous apparitions of Athena that occurred within the temple: the first during the Persian Wars when the goddess promised to intercede with Zeus; the second giving instructions concerning the proper steps to be followed after the pollution of the sanctuary caused by a person's suicide there; and the third (which were repeated appearances) during the siege of Rhodes by Demetrius Poliorcetes in 305–4 in which the goddess counseled seeking the help of Ptolemy of Egypt. Both for what it reveals of the 'historicising' cast of the Hellenistic mind and its emerging concern for 'documentary' authority and record, as well as for what it tells us about cultic practice and experience in the Greek world, the *Chronicle* is a uniquely important document.

From the Terastoön and the Ancient theatre, it is a short walk down to the **harbour of Aghios Pavlos**, where St Paul is thought to have landed on Rhodes. Looking back towards the Acropolis from here, the wide, arching cave which undercuts the rock directly below the Temple of Athena is visible. Its name—**Panaghia Spiliotissa** (Virgin of the Cave)—indicates that it was a place of early Christian worship, which followed a preceding pagan cult. The walls of the cave bear a late inscription of the 3rd century AD, with the name and title of one of the priests of Athena *Lindia*, Lucius Aelius Aglochartos—perhaps the same individual who added the inscription to the exedra at the entrance to the acropolis, mentioned above.

Round the opposite side of the acropolis-rock, beyond the limits of the lower town and on the slope approximately 100m north/northeast of the acropolis, is a site referred to as the ***Boukopeíon***—a 'place for the sacrifice of oxen'. A large number of visible Archaic (6th century BC) **inscriptions** on the surfaces of the rocks on the ground reveal the area to have had early cultic significance. Vestiges of foundations show there to have been also a sizeable temple of the Geometric period here (10th century BC). Some scholars have conjectured that this is the site of the unusual 'fire-less sacrifice' to which Pindar enigmatically refers in his *7th Olympian Ode* (l. 48) in connection with Lindos. The sacrifice of oxen unconsummated by fire would certainly be anomalous in the ancient world: equally plausible as an explanation, is that 'fire-less' sacrifice may refer simply to offerings of grain and fruit.

In the face of the **Hill of Kraná** behind the town, due west of the acropolis—and clearly visible from it, just above the upper line of the area of habitation—is a ruined Hellenistic chamber-tomb known as the **Tomb of Archokrates**, dating from c. 200 BC. (*Access—difficult—is from the southwest corner of the town.*) The tomb is now very decayed, although in front of the entrance there is a well-preserved row of four carved altars, bearing the names of the dead. These were originally placed on the deep rock-cut ledge above the entrance, to which access was gained from the hill above. Originally the mausoleum would have presented an impressive 23m façade, formed by a Doric colonnade with decorated frieze above and pilastered wings to either side; this created a monumental entrance to the funerary chamber which was cut into the hillside.

More distant, and magnificently sited on the extremity of the northern cape of the 'Great Harbour' north of Lindos, is the circular monument known as the '**Tomb of Cleoboulos**'. This is reached by a 30-minute walk which is rewarding for its tranquility and its fine views of Lindos. (*From a signed junction half way down the road to the beach from the main plateia at the edge of the town, a path leads out onto the headland.*) The terrain is rough and rocky but carpeted in different seasons with asphodel or saffron-bearing crocus, and punctuated by a few tenacious pomegranate trees. The footpath passes beside another monument to Ioannis Zidgis above the bay; half way along the headland are a couple of **windmills**, one of which is well-preserved, with a doorstep in marble taken from an ancient building. On the southern tip of the headland, is the circular 'tomb' (9m in diameter and c. 1.70m high) conspicuously marking the entrance to the natural harbour above a steep drop into the sea. Its fine

masonry—well-finished blocks of Lardos marble, regular in form, but not of identical size—and the meticulous precision of its construction would suggest building work of the 4th or 3rd century BC—certainly later than the (Archaic) age of Cleoboulos (*see below*). At the corners of the entrance the stone is pleasingly drafted: below and to the right is the projection of part of the threshold. A cross engraved above the door records that the building was used in mediaeval times as a church dedicated to Aghios Aimilianos. The building may not actually be a tomb, even though this remains a probable hypothesis: its similarity to the bases of other Hellenistic towers in the area, and in particular to the lighthouse tower of Akeratos on Thasos, would point to other possible interpretations of its function, which do not necessarily exclude a funerary element: the tower on Thasos, for example, was both a monument to Akeratos as well as a functioning signal-point and lighthouse. Tradition alone has connected the building with Lindos's most famous citizen, and since his name occurs several times in this text it may be worth saying a word here about who Cleoboulos was.

CLEOBOULOS AND THE 'SEVEN SAGES'

A figure of patriarchal wisdom, combining valour, humility and moderation, Cleoboulos was considered one of the 'Seven Sages'—a loosely defined grouping of early Greek thinkers and doers, revered for their wisdom and first recorded as being seven in number by Plato. The group included (in addition to Cleoboulos): Thales of Miletus, Byas of Priene, Pittacus of Mytilene, Solon of Athens, Chilon of Sparta and Periander of Corinth. Herodotus gives several instances of their pragmatism and political acuity in Book I of his *Histories*. Cleoboulos appears to have been an enlightened leader of Lindos in the early decades of the 6th century BC, and presided over the city's period of greatest prestige and prosperity. He may have had considerable contact with Solon of Athens; he was a talented poet, and like many of his generation had travelled to, and felt the influence of, Egypt and her culture. The immortal guiding epithet, 'Nothing in excess', which was inscribed at the entrance to the Oracle at Delphi, is attributed to him.

CENTRAL RHODES AND THE THREE MOUNTAINS

The centre of the island is a relatively wild and wooded landscape, neither much visited nor overly affected by modern construction. To the west side it is dominated by the three mountains of Mount Prophítis Elías (780m), Mount Atávyros (1,216m) and Mount Akramýtis (823m)—in effect three peaks of the same massif; to the east, deeply folded valleys of pine woods and olives slope down to the coast, their waters draining down wide, seasonal torrents. The mountains are of pure limestone, while the eastern valleys have an often pale, sandy alluvial soil and sandstone features. This contrast creates a wide range of habitats for plants and animals.

AROUND MOUNT PROPHITIS ELIAS

The curious, semi-abandoned hill-top village of **Eleoúsa** (37.5km from Rhodes), created by the Italians as the 'Campochiaro Agricultural Settlement' in 1935, at the eastern end of Mount Prophítis Elías can be reached either from the west coast at Soroní (25km from Rhodes) via the monastery chapel and spring of Aghios Soulas, or from the junction (22km) on the main east-coast road south of Afándou, via Archipolis. Either approach leads through particularly rich agricultural lands.

By a series of scarcely-veiled laws of expropriation passed between 1924 and 1929, the Italians systematically transferred the island's agricultural production from the local Greek population to Italian settlers, and brand-new settlements were created here and at other points on the island.

'Campochiaro', as it was called then, was designed from scratch by Rodolfo Petracco and Armando Bernabiti in 1935/6, with less felicitous outcome than the project for Porto Lago on Leros on which they also worked together. Roads wind up to the main hippodrome-shaped *piazza* which stretches between the Church and the School at opposite ends. To either side are the settlement's *administration buildings* with their characteristic 'submerged' arcades and, at times capricious, architectural juxtapositions. These are not unattractive creations, and they use the same design-vocabulary as the architects' other buildings in the city; but they remain fundamentally divorced from the rural landscape around. After the Italians left, the Greeks re-named the settlement after an attribute of the Virgin, '*eleousa*'—'compassionate': they returned to the cultivation of the land and abandoned the ostentatious buildings to the ruin of time. An unreal atmosphere prevails, relieved and rendered elegiac by the shade of the now mature umbrella pines and palm trees.

The road west along the mountain ridge passes at the edge of the settlement of Eleoúsa an unexpectedly large fountain pool (originally also used for swimming) designed by the Italian architects for a rising spring of water. Its simple, low circularity is of considerable elegance.

Two kilometres to the west, beside another *spring of remarkably soft water, is the characterful *church of Aghios Nikolaos 'Foundoukli' ('of the hazelnut'), beautiful both in itself and in its panoramic and bucolic site.

This is a domed 14th century votive chapel built on a Greek-cross plan which has been extended with apses to give the impression of a quatrefoil. It measures no more than 8 m x 8 m and is surmounted by an attractively arcaded cupola decorated with knotted pilasters and a belfry above the west door. Unusually, there are doors also to north and south, as though the building were a baptistery. Its design makes it a rural cousin of St George in the Old City—with rougher masonry and less gracious proportions, but with great charm nonetheless. The space created within and the form from without are both captivating. Unlike St George it preserves, almost complete, the cycle of **wall-paintings** of its interior which were executed perhaps a century or more after the church's construction: an earlier layer may lie beneath. The dome, which was rebuilt at the beginning of the 20th century, no longer has its Pantocrator figure; but virtually every other surface is covered—from the *Evangelists* in the squinches, down through the ***Scenes of the Life and Passion of Christ***, to the row of saints who stand at ground-level here and with whom one has the pleasing sensation of mixing at ease in the small space. The narrative scenes are conceived with clarity and liveliness and show slight Italian influence. Beside the west door is the ***dedicatory scene*** with the donors and their family presenting a model of the church to Christ.

The continuation of the beautifully wooded road to the west (right hand branch after 1.5km) leads towards the summit of Prophítis Elías. At 6km from Aghios Nikolaos, are two more unexpected curiosities of the Italian occupation: in a Tyrolean chalet-style of architecture, are two hotel buildings—the main, **Eláfos** ('**Stag**') **Hotel** (1928) and the **Elafína** ('**Doe**') (1930) designed by Rodolfo Petracco to provide a place of recreation, or '*villeggiatura*', for the Italian settlers who were far from, and nostalgic for, a week-end in Cortina d'Ampezzo. Other buildings in similar style are to be found on the mountain further to the west. Just to the east of the Elafos Hotel is the small, whitewashed monastery of the Prophet Elijah.

Of all the island's mountains, Prophítis Elías has perhaps the richest **flora**. Its mature woods of pine and cypress are favoured by drifts of wild flowers in the clearings—large quantities of cyclamen, in particular—an endemic, Rhodian *Cyclamen repandum rhodense*, and *Cyclamen persicum*. This area is also home to the beautiful **wild peony** with wide, enamel-white flowers formed of few petals, and with gold-yellow stamens, often touched with scarlet at the very centre. This is a Rhodian subspecies (*rhodia*) of the *Paeonia clusii* found otherwise only on Crete and Karpathos. The flower (March/April) has a light cinnamon perfume.

Wild orchids of many varieties are also prolific. Much rarer and harder to see is the endemic, delicate yellow, Rhodian fritillary. Both common and long-legged buzzard (the latter, distinguished by its ruddier hue and a tail with no markings on the under side) are resident year-round and are often seen hunting from the sky.

To north and south, respectively, of the ridge are the two attractive villages of **Sálakos** (31km)—where there are abundant springs, two Byzantine churches of the 14th and 15th centuries and the remains of a fortress—and **Apóllona** (44km), reached by a panoramic descent of the south side of the mountain. There is a small **museum** in the centre of the latter, exhibiting domestic artefacts, folk art and a selection of ancient pieces—sarcophagi and altars decorated with garlands and *bucrania*. A section of Byzantine wall stands in the forecourt, which was part of a destroyed church.

A long and deeply rural road (18km, un-surfaced) leads through uninhabited valleys, densely wooded with Calabrian pine, due south from Apóllona to **Láerma** (63km). Both villages, as well as the monastery of Artamíti to the west of their mid-point, and the town of Asklipieío to the south, have names probably relating to the cults of the ancient gods: Apollo, Hermes, Artemis and Asklepios. 'Láerma' ('Ladarma') is thought to represent a corruption of '*laos Ermís*' ('people of Hermes'). Empty though this landscape has always been, the tutelary deities watched over it from all sides.

AROUND MONI THARRI

In a peaceful setting 4km to the southwest of Láerma is the oldest monastic foundation on the island, and still one of the most active today: the monastery of the Archangel Michael '*Tharrinos*', or '**Moni Tharri**' (67km). (*Open continuously until sunset.*) The foundation may go back as far as the 9th century; the main *catholicon* building is of the early 12th century; and there are ***wall-paintings** in several layers, dating principally from the 13th, 15th and 17th centuries—all of considerable quality. The monastery was rescued from decline in 1990 by the efforts of a new abbot from Patmos, and the stable monastic community of mostly (young) Greek and Serbian monks now numbers over twenty.

The church is cruciform with two short arms and a long nave, surmounted by an arcaded cupola-drum. The west door is curiously off-centre, perhaps because of the position of the threshold in a pre-existing structure (whose foundations can be seen to the north side of the church). Many periods of painting are represented in the impressive interior: the austere figures of the *Church Fathers* in the lowest area in the apse are probably contemporary with the construction of the church (12th century); those in the dome, drum, vault and sanctuary walls—the (damaged) *Pantocrator*, the *Virgin, St John the Baptist, Angels and Prophets*—are slightly later work of the early 13th century. It should be recalled that a later layer of 17th century paintings which originally covered these was removed and is now displayed inside the church of St Mary of the Castle, in Rhodes (*see pp. 81–82*). An inscription in the *prothesis* niche to the left side of the sanctuary, dates the paintings of the upper cylinder of the apse to 1506. In the arms of the church the *Archangels* (south), *SS Demetrius and George* (north) and the scenes of the *Annunciation* (with donor) and *Dormition* (north) are also of the 16th century. The **Scenes of the Life of Christ* along the vault of the nave, although the latest—early 18th century—are in many ways the most remarkable: the style of the artist is quite individual and would seem to show his training as a manuscript illuminator. Line-drawing prevails over modelling in all the scenes, and details of costume or background are delicately described as if with a fine-pen. The effect is most unusual; the compositions—*Christ and the Woman of Samaria*, *The Angel at the Empty Sepulchre*, *The Storm on the Sea of Galilee*—are beautifully balanced and executed by an artist of considerable talent. The finely carved wooden iconostasis is also work of the early 18th century.

Sixteen kilometres of winding, wooded track leads down from Moni Tharri to the east coast via the monastery's dependent foundations—the contemporaneous **Aghios Giorgios Inkou**, and the 19th century convent of the **Panaghia Ypsenís**.

KRITINIA AND AROUND MOUNT ATAVYROS

The **Castle of Kritinía** (53km), often just referred to as '**Kastellos**', is the largest of the Knights' fortresses along the island's west coast. From its cliff-side position, high (130m) above emerald water, 1.5km southwest of the harbour of Skala Kameirou, it dominates the western passage and the channel of Chalki, and has fine views beyond to Tilos, Symi and Nisyros.

> The walls on the landward side are well-preserved with three imposing towers—one rectangular, one polygonal, and one circular. Both the joins of the masonry and the coats of arms here—Grand Masters Pierre d'Aubusson (main block) and Emery d'Amboise and Fabrizio del Carretto (eastern wing)—are evidence that the structure was raised in several successive campaigns of building between 1478 and 1521. Though its principal purpose must have been for look-out and signalling, the ruins of a large collapsed chapel (bearing the royal arms of France on one of the quoins) and three cisterns in the centre, suggest the presence of a fairly large permanent garrison.

The village of **Kritinía** (55km) itself is attractively sited in a panoramic hollow of the hills above, around a plane shaded *plateia* with a small fountain (commemorating Captain Federico Marozzo della Rocca, veteran of the 1916 Italian campaigns in Friuli). The **folklore museum** above the village by the main road has a wide variety of local kinds of earthenware and pottery, urns and storage *pithoi*.

Beyond Kritinía, the road climbs rapidly towards the flank of **Mount Atávyros** (1,216m), the island's highest, bulkiest and—in Antiquity—most sacred, mountain. Above 800m altitude its long ridge is bare limestone; below, it is densely wooded in pine and (to the north side) in oak and chestnut. The **ascent to the *summit** of Aghios Ioannis can be made either from the south in a relatively gradual, five to six hour (return) climb from the village of Aghios Isidoros, or else by road and military track (leading to the NATO installation at the summit) from the junction 5km south of the (southern exit of) Kritinía, which climbs through the pine forests in the saddle between the two peaks of the mountain and approaches Aghios Ioannis from the south west. Either way the effort is amply rewarded if the weather is clear by the sight of one of the most dramatically placed sanctuaries in the Aegean. The whole island lies beneath; Crete is visible to the southwest and Asia Minor to the northeast.

It is said that Althaemenes, son of Catreus, King of Crete, fled to Rhodes after a frightening oracular prediction and settled on the island, founding a **temple to Zeus *Atabyrios*** on the only point on the island from which his homeland could clearly be seen. He brought with him many settlers from Crete; the name of the village above the coast below— Kritinía, or *Cretenia* in Antiquity—may derive from this. At *Acragas* (Agrigento) in Sicily, Zeus *Atabyrios* was worshipped together with Athena, whose cult may also have been present on the mountaintop here. A number of figurines of bulls have been found at this site, and ancient sources refer to the presence of large bronze bulls in the sanctuary which were wont to bellow and groan when some ill-fate was approaching.

The extensive remains are clearly visible on the ridge 500m to the southeast of the military radar tower. The large rectangular base (c. 15m x 11m) of a structure, surrounded by a ***peribolos*** of about 40m square, occupies the top of the ridge. Below to the north east side is the 20m long **base of a stoa** or portico in four courses of rusticated ashlar blocks of probably 5th century workmanship, with what appears to be a water-pool at its western end. Elements of other structures fill the space between the two areas. A number of meticulously cut and carved architectural elements lie all round, including blocks and pedestals bearing dowel-holes and what appears to be a lustral basin. Yet there is no evidence of columns or entablature suggesting a temple. What was here probably partook more of the nature of a **large altar** (oriented perfectly east/west) than of an actual temple. The grey stone was quarried on the saddle just below the rise to the west. The name of the summit Aghios Ioannis, suggests the ruins were 'Christianised' at some point as a chapel; but no visible evidence of this remains.

Constructing, visiting, even conceiving of a sanctuary in such a place so arduous of access, is a measure of the enduring freedom of the Ancient Greek imagination. If the Divine and Invisible were present to them in even such a daunting place, no thought was given to mere human convenience in honouring that presence. The site, to be properly understood, needs to be visited by foot in a storm, as the peak is enveloped in the thunder and lightning of Zeus.

On the fertile lower slopes of the northern side of the mountain are some of the island's most renowned vines. The sprawling settlement of **Embonas** (62km) is the principal centre for wine production; the C.A.I.R. co-operative is based here which produces a variety of wines—amongst which is Greece's only *méthode champenoise* wine. Production of a less commercial nature continues also on the southern slopes at **Aghios Isidoros**, a tranquil village backed by the massif of the mountain and over-looking an ocean of pine-clad hills descending to the sea towards the east.

AROUND MOUNT AKRAMYTIS

The short stretch of *panoramic road between Mount Atávyros and Mount Akramýtis is the most dramatic on the island. Five hundred metres after passing the second turning for Embonas, as you come from Kritinía, the view which opens out over forests, sea and islands to the north is worth pausing for. At a hairpin bend shortly after, the road crosses a fissure in the rocks, carved by seasonal torrents descending from the mountain, whose sides are formed with tightly-packed horizontal striations to which trees cling improbably: in the vicinity are depos-its of the purple-red stone used at points in the ancient structures of *Ialysos* and *Lindos*. After a further 4.5km, (1.5km before entering Siána) a track leads west (right) to **Steliés** (69km), and the empty, southern loop of Mount Akramytis. Although little explored, there is a large area here—designated with the ancient name '**Kymisala**'—with widely scattered remains of habitation from the Classical and Hellenistic periods.

One kilometre down the track from the junction, on the right hand side, is an open area where the bases of stone walls of houses and other structures, constructed in large blocks, can be seen. There is considerable overlay of later use, however, and the ancient blocks have in several places been re-arranged in circles so as to create winnowing areas. Five hundred metres further on is a small church of the Zoödochos Pigi: this overlooks a spur on which there are more remains of ancient walls, and the base of a collapsed **tower** (centre) and **perimeter wall** can be seen. Of greatest interest are a number of **blocks bearing eroded inscriptions** in large letters, which are to be found to the southwest, roughly in the middle of the brow overlooking the deep, cultivated 'basin' below. The latter has the appearance of a small drained lake, and must have been an important element in the choice of ancient settlement here.

Beyond this point, the track skirts the wooded north and west sides of Mount Akramytis and eventually loops back to Monólithos, affording beautiful views towards the island of Chalki along the route. The main asphalted road follows the southern slope of the mountain to the same point via **Siána** (71km), a straggling village of stone houses with an enviable south-facing position commanding views down to the tip of the island and beyond. The village is famous for its local products of aromatic honey and '*souma*'—a spirit similar to Italian *grappa*. The centre is dominated by the modern church of Aghios Panteleímonas: its 15th century predecessor, a low, barrel-vaulted, stone structure stands inconspicuously to its west—attractive from outside but bare inside. The villages of Siána and Monólithos (76km) lie in an area rich in archaeology—especially burials and funerary finds: in the latter, a mid 6th century BC cremation-pyre containing over 40 vases was excavated in the 1940s near the school building. There is also continuity of habitation into mediaeval times: to the west of the village's main church is the 15th century **Aghios Thomás**, which conserves paintings in patches in the upper areas of its walls.

The fortress, or **Castle of Monólithos** (78km), from which the village takes its name, is 2km further to the southwest. It is in effect a fortified, precipitous rock—referred to as the 'Monópetra'—with sheer sides dropping 200m to the valley below and with access from only one point by means of a precarious neck of land. The position commands the approaches to the island from the south. This was primarily a watch-tower and signalling post; its interior area is therefore compact and its cisterns sufficient only to supply a small garrison. Of the two chapels inside, one is in ruins, the other, **Aghios Panteleímonas**, recently restored. The (latest) phase of building here is once again the work of the energetic Pierre d'Aubusson. His master plan must have conceived of the whole island as one huge, single fortress, anchored like a ship in the sea, to be defended with a cage of impregnable castles around its shores.

SOUTHERN RHODES

The southern tip of the island is a spacious and panoramic landscape bordered by long sandy shores. Its central hills are surrounded by a good circuit-road linking the main settlements of Gennádi, Apolakkiá and Kattavía. The itinerary described here begins at the main junction at Kálathos, west of Lindos, where the section on the northeast of the island ended, covers the sites of interest inside and outside the loop of the circuit road, and finishes at the island's southernmost tip.

PILONAS, LARDOS AND ASKLIPIEIO

West of the main junction at Kalathos (42km from Rhodes) just north of Lindos, the road climbs for 2km to Pilónas; at the summit of the rise is the 15th century church of **Aghios Giorgios** whose north interior wall has paintings in deteriorating condition. A right turn off the main road is signed to the **Mycenaean cemetery of Asprópilia** which was excavated between 1993–96. This consists of six tombs, two with side-chambers cut into the soft sandstone rock, dating from the late Mycenaean period—14th-12th centuries BC. Each is entered by a *dromos* or entrance gallery on the same, almost due-south, axis. Finds made here include pottery—much of it imported from the Argolid in the Peloponnese—and glass paste beads of Egyptian manufacture.

The village of **Lárdos** (46.5km), which has given its name to the mottled **grey marble** quarried in the area, is an important junction at the crossing of a seasonal river and is the main market-town of a large hinterland to the north. A fortress which substantially predates the Knights' presence on Rhodes guards it from the hills to the southwest. It was this fortress and its estates in the valley below that the Genoese adventurer, Vignolo de' Vignoli, who already had a foothold on the island, was to receive for his personal use as part of his reward for his military support in helping the Knights take Rhodes from the Byzantine Empire in 1306–9.

The coastal road south of the village passes between

the shore and low cliffs which are visibly shaped and perforated by the marble quarries both of Antiquity and of
more recent times. These are the last limestone outcrops
encountered as the road heads south; beyond, the landscape changes, sweeping down to the sea in folds of softer,
formless sandstone. At 55km (13km from the Kalathos
junction), a turning inland leads 3.5km to **Asklipieío**,
similarly guarded by a conspicuous fortress of the Hospitaller period. The village's treasure is the 11th century
church of the Dormition, or 'Koimisis tis Theotokou', in
the central square, whose magnificent *painted interior
is comparable with the church of the Panaghia in Lindos
and with Moni Tharri for the completeness and beauty
of its decoration (*often locked outside times of liturgies; the
custodian in the house directly to the south keeps the key*).
The church, which dates from 1060, has been cleaned
externally and the masonry re-pointed: the discontinu-
ity in the stonework on the west façade shows from outside how two aisles to north and south have been added
in the 18th century onto the central nave of the original
cruciform church: this original structure may also have
evolved in two phases, beginning as a Greek cross plan,
and then being modified into a Latin cross plan by addition to the west arm. This becomes clearer once inside
the long, low interior, which is paved with a *chochlakia*

mosaic floor and covered on all sides with wall-paintings of the late 16th century.

The whole range of Scripture is here, from *Genesis* to the *Revelation*, disposed around the walls with the meticulous 'universal' logic typical of Byzantine church designs. The *Pantocrator* in the celestial circle of the dome; the *Evangelists*, as transmitters of divine wisdom in the pendentives; the *Virgin and Child* in the conch of the apse; scenes relating to mortality in the transepts—the *Apocalypse* and the *Virgin's Dormition* to the south; a dramatically large and solemn *Archangel Michael* clasping a shrouded human soul in his hand, and *Herod's Massacre of the Innocents* to the north; then, along the vault of the nave, the *Fall from Grace* related in the scenes from Genesis, mirrored by the *Redemption* through the Life of Christ. All this swirls above us, while—standing at our level, are the reassuring intercessors—*St John the Baptist* and *St George* in their own niches to either side of the congregational area, and the other saints ranged around. Most splendidly dressed of all are *SS. Constantine and Helen* in the north arm. As we exit to the world outside, images of the *Last Judgement* around the door in the west wall act as a salutary warning. A perfect whole—more memorable for its completeness as a decorative cycle than for the particular quality of the painting.

A small **Ecclesiastical Museum** and, next to it, a **Folklore Museum** are housed in the adjacent buildings to the south.

From the vantage point of the small early 15th century **castle** above, the plan and development of the church below is clear. The fortress itself is considerably ruined, but its two cylindrical towers survive and a very deep, irregularly shaped cistern in the centre of the compound still conserves its impermeable lining. A number of small churches can be seen dotting the landscape all around the village. The most interesting of these is **Aghios Giorgios Labra** which lies below the village to the south, a little above the river course. In a niche in the north wall is a mural of the *Virgin and Child*: the quality of the simple modelling and definition of the face and the blessing hand of the Virgin is noteworthy. The altar of the chapel is a re-used antique capital.

THE AREA OF VATI, PROPHILIA, ARNITHA AND APOLAKKIA

At the junction (58.5km) in **Gennádi**, 3.5km further south along the east coast road from the turning to Asklepieío, a road cuts west across the tip of the island to Apolakkiá and the southwest coast. 2.5km inland on this road is **Váti**, a small village with a picturesque main square of stone houses, which is at the centre of a hilly landscape, ideal for exploration on foot. In the valley to the east of the village a Mycenaean necropolis has been uncovered. There are several ruined windmills in the vicinity and many rural churches—some with wall-paintings, some with ancient marbles as altars, some decorated only in the last few years. The most remarkable church in the area, however, is in the village of **Prophilía**, 6.5 km to the north, which hugs the ridge of a hill with distant views of the sea. Beside the road in the centre of the village is the 12th century **church of SS. Michael and George**—a small, vaulted space with *****paintings of the late 12th century** of the highest quality, in a fresh and vigorous style which is seen in few other places on the island. The spare lines of the figures, and in particular the compelling faces and eyes of the protagonists (Christ, John the Baptist, the Virgin) are marvellous examples of art of the Comnene age—one of the last periods of Byzantine art before an unhappy fossilisation of forms sets in. For this author, at least, these are the finest paintings on the island.

On the north wall (symbolically the side of Satan, from which evil comes) are the saints who defend us from that evil: St Anthony, and the two mounted **figures of St George**

and the Archangel Michael, beautifully conceived in relation to one another. (Note also St George's square stirrups.) Above is the *Crucifixion* and the *Harrowing of Hell*. What dominates the interior, however, is the powerful ***face of the Pantocrator**** in the conch, between His Mother and St John the Baptist. On the arch above, an almost monochrome ***Almighty in a nimbus***, framed by angels boldly and beautifully depicted in flight, points to His Son below and to the Virgin Mary to one side, who accepts the acclaim with innocence and dignity. On the south side the scenes from the *Life of the Virgin* and from the Apocalypse are less well-preserved. The colours are fresh: a (ferrous oxide) yellow ochre, typical of wall-painting of the period, predominates.

By coincidence—as if to round off the pleasure given by these paintings—one of the best rural *tavernas* on Rhodes is directly opposite the church (see 'Eating' below).

The villages of **Istrio**, **Arnítha** and **Apolakkiá** to the west of here are small agricultural centres, set in a verdant and well-watered landscape, with stone houses grouped around a *plateia* and church at their centres. There are several functioning monasteries in the area, the most attractive of which is Aghios Ioannis, between Prophilía and Arnítha. Near to it is the site of **Aghia Irini** where there are remains of **two Early Christian basilicas and**

a baptistery. (*The site is in a field beyond a small grove of young olive trees, 100m west of the Arnítha to Istrio road, at a point which is 30m north of the sign to the monastery of Aghios Ioannis, as you come from Arnítha.*) There are the remains of at least two (?) 6th century churches standing to over 2m in height in places. One, to the south of the area, has a double apse; the larger one to the north, has its *synthronon* still visible as well as the base of the altar and its canopy. There are several columns in fine, local marble within the area of the ruins; just to the west, in the field, are fragments of a large water-stoup or font, and other pieces of worked stone. To the north is the floor of a **tetraconch baptistery** with **mosaic floor**, figuring both abstract patterns and designs with birds. It is difficult to assess how large the site once was; shards—predominantly of *pithoi* and storage vases—litter the area for some distance around.

From the east side of the village of Apolakkiá, a track leads off to the north towards a water-reservoir and dam. After 3km a turn left leads up a steep slope to the isolated church of **Aghios Giorgios Vardas**—a simple, single-aisled building whose **paintings** inside can be dated precisely to 1289/90 from the donor's inscription. Even though their condition is not good, many of the scenes are legible: *Christ's Entry into Jerusalem* (south side), and some of the figures of saints, such as *St Tryphon and St Nikitas* (northwest corner), stand out in particular. Their quality is good, but they have no great originality: a moment's comparison with those in Prophilía shows how that 'fossilisation' had taken hold in the hundred years that separate these two cycles.

MESANAGROS

The landscape south of Apolakkiá is one of eroded sandstone, whose sharp ridges look like waves whipped into peaks by the sea. The presence of rounded rocks and stones a considerable distance inland suggests that it was not long ago that the area was under the sea. The long sandy beaches and dunes on both coasts are attractive, but often windswept. Four kilometres inland of the west coast-road is **Moni Skiadi** which, although originally an 11th century foundation (c. 1060), was re-built in 1877. Its unusual name is a corruption of '*Skitiádi*' or '*Mikrí Skíti*', meaning a 'small cloister'. Six kilometres to its east along an un-surfaced track through an empty landscape is the village of Mesanagrós, set on a strategic inland ridge as a refuge from coastal piracy in the Dark Ages. The 13th century *church of the Dormition at the entrance to the village rises over the floor of a much larger **5th century,**

Early Christian basilica; its apse fits snugly into that of the older building. The latter was decorated with **mosaic floors**: there are abstract designs visible outside in the south *parecclesion*; and an area of roundels with birds to the northwest of the existing church. There is also an area of patterned, brick-tile floor. A marble column from the basilica set on its side forms the **lintel** of the doorway of the existing church. The interior is a single—unusually wide and low—vault which springs from re-used, early Christian capitals and columns, with small areas of the 5th century marble floor under foot. A magnificent, free-standing **baptismal font** fashioned from a single block of marble stands in the middle of the floor, bearing its Byzantine inscription referring to the redeeming power of the Saviour through baptism.

In the valley 2.5km below Mesanagrós, on the north side of the road to Lachaniá, is the 14th century chapel of **Aghios Thomás**, with buttress blocks to its north and south sides. There are darkened paintings inside: to either side of a painted altar table decked with monstrance and salver in the apse, stand SS. Paul and Nikitas. Beyond the church, the road subsequently descends to **Lachaniá**, in whose main plateia are two fine fountains, one with Ottoman inscription.

KATTAVIA AND THE SOUTHERN TIP OF THE ISLAND

The shallow waters around the southern tip of the island are a habitat of both green and **loggerhead turtles**, which may still breed in the vicinity of the promontory of Cape Germatá, due south of Chóchlakas. This was considered one of their last breeding places in the Dodecanese. The dunes and areas of garrigue by the shore in this southeast corner are also rich in **bird-life** and **flowers**. King Ferdinand's orchid (*Ophrys regis-fernandii*)—unflatteringly known as the 'earwig orchid', because its dark elongated lip has the slick texture and form of an earwig's body and head—is endemic to this corner of the Aegean and can often be found here, together with others, such as the holy- and pyramidal- orchids. Larks, swallows (including red-rumped swallows, recognisable by the russet and white patch above the dark tail), and both black-headed and Cretzschmar's buntings, breed in the area; in periods of migration, there is a wide variety of song-birds and waders.

At the northern end of Plimiri Bay is the church of the **Zoödochos Pigi**, a 16th century building incorporating **ancient columns** and capitals in its structure: tombs and part of a circuit wall can be seen on the landward side of the promontory above the church. A very different kind of church is to be seen 4.5km west of Chóchlakas beside the main road—the disused concrete structure of the church of **Aghios Pavlos**, formerly the Catholic church of the Italian **Agricultural Settlement of San Marco** (Petracco and Bernabiti, 1936). The long horizontal lines of the settlement's administrative buildings, broken only by the vault and the tower of the church, are reminiscent of structures in the Tuscan Maremma where agricultural buildings in similar style and of the same period are to be found. The broad brick surround of the church's west door recalls the Catalan door-frames in the Old City of Rhodes.

Kattavía (76km from Rhodes) has the feel of 'the end of the line': many of its fine houses are abandoned or ruined; the main church and school, as if to compensate, have been over-restored. The village was fortified by the Knights of St John to provide a safe refuge for the local population in an area very susceptible to pirate attack, but nothing now remains to be seen of these walls. Mycenaean tombs have been found in the vicinity of the village, and there is evidence of a Late Bronze Age settlement here on the spur of Aghios Minás. Finds of later Greek and Roman pottery show that occupation continued into historic times. The principal archaeological remains in the area, however, are to be seen at the very extremity of the island, 9km to the south across a deserted area now occupied mostly by the Military. The track to the right (west) just in front of the isthmus of the islet of Prasonísi, leads to the foot of a sloping promontory, on which are the remains of **Ancient *Vrouliá***, a Late Geometric/Early Archaic settlement (8th to 6th centuries BC). Most of what is of interest to the visitor lies on the far side of the hill. A wall runs northwest/southeast along the ridge and the stepped or terraced foundations of the ancient houses run along this axis. At the summit, with good views of Karpathos and beyond, the remains of the most substantial building lie athwart the main axis and are oriented east/west, suggesting a probable cultic use. Beyond, at the northwestern extremity, is a sheer drop to the sea below. The site has given its name to a distinctive style of Archaic, black-figure pottery, in which floral designs are lightly incised into the dark surface and colours added afterwards.

The **islet of Prasonísi** (with a lighthouse on its far side) is tethered to the main island by a narrow isthmus, which defines two sweeping sandy bays to either side, one or other of which takes the force of any wind blowing, creating conditions ideal for the dedicated surfer. The meagre settlement by the isthmus and its lodgings are mostly given over to the pursuit of this hobby in the summer season. In the winter there is nobody; and the sunsets—and even the surf—can be more dramatic.

PRACTICAL INFORMATION

851 00-09 Rhodes: area 1,401sq. km; perimeter 220km; resident population 115,334; max. altitude 1,216m. **Port Authority**: 22410 22220, 28888, 28666. **Travel and information**: www.travel-rhodes.com

ACCESS

By air: With a total of 6–7 daily flights from Athens to Rhodes operated by both Olympic Air and Aegean Airways, Rhodes is easily accessible at all times of year. Its airport is also the hub for local flights within the area to Kastellorizo, Karpathos and Kasos (almost daily), and to Kos, Leros and Astypalaia (three times weekly). There are also daily connections direct to Thessaloniki and to Heraklion (Crete). The air-port is 15km southwest of the centre of Rhodes town (€15 by taxi).

By boat: The port of Rhodes is also the principal hub for the Dodecanese Islands, with daily connections to all the principal islands, though the frequency of connections to the lesser islands varies considerably according to season (see entries for individual islands). There are year-round, direct connections by car-ferry to Piraeus (c. 16 hours) every day; and connections to eastern Crete twice weekly. In the holiday season, there are also daily connections (by private carriers) to Marmaris in Turkey. Since the port is large and has several harbours, it is important to ascertain from which part of it a ferry will leave. The neighbouring island of Chalki is served twice weekly from Rhodes town, but there is a daily service from Kameiros Skala (2 hours). The GNTO office in the New Town (corner of Makariou and Papagou Streets, T. 22410 44335) provides helpful sheets with weekly boat departures, museum opening times, a price-list for taxis and schedules of bus times and fares for the whole island. Its web-site is www.ando.gr/eot

LODGING

The most beautiful and characterful place to stay in the Old Town of Rhodes is the *Hotel Marco Polo (T./fax 22410 25562, www. marcopolomansion@web.com; open May–late Oct) at 42 Aghiou Phanaríou Street, not far from where it joins (the main) Sokrátous Street at the Mehmet Agha Mosque. With architecturally fine rooms of great individuality, and the thoughtful and friendly service that goes with private ownership, this is a memorable place either to stay or just to dine on its imaginative, traditional food in the peace and quiet of a mediaeval walled-garden. Elegant, modern luxury at a higher price, in an enviable location just off the Street of the Knights, is offered by the newly opened *Avalon Boutique Hotel (*T./fax 22410 31438/31439, www.avalonrhodes.gr*), which is open all year round. The Old Town also has many small and characterful pensions: worthy of mention are, **The Apollo Guesthouse** (*T. 22410 32003, www.apollo-touristhouse.com*) and **Hotel Andreas** (*T. 22410 34156, fax 74285, www.hotelandreas.com*), at 28c and 28d Omírou Street respectively (contiguous, but under separate management) not far from the St John/Koskinou Gate, and overlooking the ancient church of Aghia Kyriaki. Both are relatively inexpensive, and inhabit interesting buildings; the rooms are comfortable, but small. At Ippodámou Street,

61, is the delightful **S. Nikolis Hotel** (*T. 22410 34561, fax 32034, www.s-nikolis.gr*). These last three close between late October and the week before Easter. In the winter season, the New Town has a number of hotels which are open year-round and offer more conventional services and convenience. Comfortable and satisfactory, without being too big or expensive, is the A-class **Hotel Mediterranean** (*T. 22410 24661, fax 22828, www.mediterranean.gr*), opposite the Casino at 35 Kos Street; most rooms have good sea-views. Exceptional value year-round is represented by the **Esperia Hotel** (*T. 22410 23941–4*) at 7 Griva Street which is warm, pleasant and strictly functional: the pool-side rooms are quietest.

EATING

Rhodes offers some of the best and most varied eating possibilities in the Aegean— although in the city itself, the visitor will need to explore outside the Old Town to sample the best Greek food. Within the walls of the Old Town, unimaginative and often overpriced tourist-fare prevails; we would suggest only: the *Marco Polo (*see lodging, above*); **Dinoris Restaurant** (*upper medium price*) in a tiny alley across from the entrance to the Archaeological Museum— an elegant and traditional taverna of long standing, one of the few in the Old Town regularly frequented by locals; **Photis Restaurant** (*expensive; open all year*) in Menekléous

Street—also an elegant and well-established fish restaurant, where the undoubted high quality and presentation of its dishes compensates for the hauteur of the reception and service. At lunchtime, *Indigo** (*medium price*), inside the Nea Agorá market-building (at no.105/6) beside Mandraki harbour, offers delicious, finely prepared dishes from the cuisine of Greek Asia Minor. Further afield (but without question worth the short taxi-ride) in Zephyros, southeast of the city centre, is the *Paragadi** fish restaurant (*medium expensive; corner of Klaude Pepper & Australias Streets: reservation recommended, T. 22410 37775*) with an exceptional quality of service and of seafood and fish dishes, prepared in the best and simplest manner. This is one of the best fish restaurants in the Dodecanese. Nearby, open all year, and usually packed with locals, is **To Steki tou Cheila** (*inexpensive*) at the southern end of Kodringtonou St., on the corner of Hadjiangelou and Dendrinou Sts: the *symiakó* (tiny shrimps) and the wine are both fresh and delicious. Around the island: **Mavrikos** in Lindos (*expensive; reservations, T. 22440 31232*) is a fine and justly famous restaurant with pleasing setting, serving many homemade products. The excellent and panoramic *To Limeri tou Listí ('The robber's den') in Prophilía (*T. 22440 61578*) in the central south of the island, certainly merits the long journey and represents one of the best places to eat on the island: it has imaginatively and carefully prepared traditional dishes of the highest standard, e.g. a light and unforgettable *imam bayaldı*. Nearby, **Petrino** in the picturesque *plateia* of Váti, is a good country taverna with fresh and unaffected cuisine.

FURTHER READING

Cecil Torr, *Rhodes in Ancient Times and Rhodes in Modern Times* (first published by CUP in 1885, both now re-issued by Archaeopress '3rd guides', Oxford); Lawrence Durrell, *Reflections on a Marine Venus* (Faber & Faber, London, 1953); H.J.A Sire, *The Knights of Malta* (Yale, London & New Haven, 1994); Vassilis Colonas, *Italian Architecture in the Dodecanese Islands, 1912–1943* (Olkos Press, Athens, 2002); Elias Kollias, *The Mediaeval City of Rhodes* etc.,(Ministry of Culture, Athens, 1998).

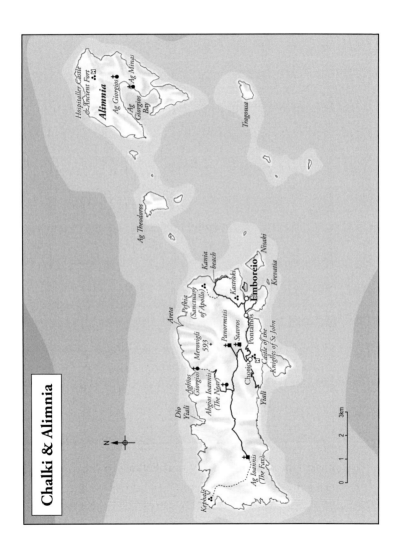

Chalki & Alimnia

Alimnia

Hospitaller Castle
& Ancient Fort

Ag Giorgios

Ag
Giorgios
Bay

Ag Minas

Tragousa

Ag Theodoros

Kania
beach

Pefkia
(Sanctuary
of Apollo)

Nisaki

Kastraki

Emboreio

Krevatia

Areta

Panormitis

Stavros

Pontamos

Merovigli
593

Aghios
Giorgios

Chorio

Castle of the
Knights of St John

Dio
Yiali

Aghios Ioannis
(The Near?)

Yiali

Ag Ioannis
(The Far?)

Kephali

N

0　　　1　　　2　　　3km

CHALKI AND ALIMNIA

Set in its own archipelago of islets off the west coast of Rhodes, Chalki is strikingly different in atmosphere from anything on Rhodes itself. The wealth once brought to this tiny, infertile island by the sponge-trade in the 19th century is immediately evident in the gracious sweep of stone houses of neoclassical inspiration that encircle the harbour: they are reminiscent of those on Symi, though not quite so patrician or so numerous. The underwater sponge-beds were the island's principal 'garden', since the harsh and waterless mountains of its interior afforded only a few oases for cultivation. Nonetheless, such 'oases' as existed were commented on long ago by Theophrastus (*Historia Plantarum*, VIII.2.9) who observed that barley would crop twice there in the same time that it took to do so once in the other islands nearby. It was perhaps on the strength of this that the island supported a relatively large population and several settlements in Antiquity, the remains of which have been found all the way from the east coast (the temple of Apollo at Pefkiá) to the island's western extremity at Cape Kepháli (where there are ruins of a Hellenistic tower), as well as in the area of the island's walled acropolis high above the centre of the south coast.

The archaeological finds—most impressive of which is a gold amphora, now in the Louvre, depicting scenes from the Trojan War—which have been found in 4th century BC tombs on the island also suggest a level of considerable prosperity. Although the island's name appears to refer to 'copper' (anc. Greek, *chalkós*), there is no remaining evidence either of the extraction or the working of the metal on the island. It is possible that the name instead derives from the Phoenician word '*karki*' meaning 'shells': indeed the island's mediaeval name, still sometimes used by mariners today, was 'Charki'.

A number of mediaeval churches with painted interiors and the fine castle of the Knights of St John are witness to the continuing importance of the island in later centuries; so, too, the dignified neoclassical architecture of the port. Chalki today is a peaceful retreat, offering un-crowded beaches, scenic walks, and both a dramatic landscape inland and an attractive seascape all around formed by its outlying islands. One of these, Alimniá, has considerable interest of its own and forms a subsection of this chapter.

HISTORY

Neolithic obsidian tools found at Kepháli in the extreme northwest of the island provide the earliest evidence of human settlement on the island. Ancient *Chalce* only steps into the pages of written texts or inscriptions in the Classical period however, first appearing in the fiscal lists of the Athenian League to which the island belonged in the 5th century BC. Thucydides cites that *Chalce* played an important role as an operations base for the Athenian fleet in 411 BC during the Peloponnesian War, against enemy ships in Rhodes. Its subsequent independence was short-lived, and the island became part of the Rhodian State in the late 4th century BC, subject to the deme of *Kameiros*. This is confirmed by Theophrastus who describes *Chalce* as a Rhodian island. Little is known of its structure or cult beyond Strabo's observation that it 'possessed a harbour and a temple of Apollo' (*Geog.* X 488). Archaeological finds from Hellenistic tombs attest considerable wealth, however.

Apart from some scattered and vestigial Early Christian remains, little is known of the island's fortunes up into the mediaeval period except that the constant danger of pirate raids forced the population to move well inland

and re-settle in the protected area of the ancient acropolis (Chorió). After the Fourth Crusade of 1204, the Venetians and Genoese re-fortified this Hellenistic acropolis. In 1366 Chalki, together with Alimniá, was granted to the Italian Assanti family. The Knights of St John subsequently rebuilt the castle on the acropolis in the mid 15th century, only to lose it in 1522/3 to the Turks, who governed the island up until 1912, when the Italians took control. Italian occupation was further confirmed by the Second Treaty of Lausanne of 1924 and became successively more restrictive and oppressive, with the compulsory imposition of Italian language. This situation resulted in the locals setting up a secret school in a cave where children were taught in Greek. The Italians surrendered to German forces in 1943. In May 1947 the island was incorporated into the Greek State together with the other islands of the Dodecanese; but it saw almost continual decline in population throughout the 20th century as those families who had worked in the sponge trade left for the United States. The émigré community of Chalkians in Tarpon Springs in Florida (which established a flourishing new sponge trade there) has nonetheless maintained strong contacts with the island and has sponsored a number of public works.

An ill-fated UNESCO scheme in 1983 to designate Chalki the 'Island of Peace and Friendship of Young People' has had disappointing results for the islanders. A modest and sustainable tourism has, however, helped to encourage the on-going restoration of the island's fine houses in recent years.

AROUND THE PORT

No careless modern construction disturbs the wide arc of dignified and regular 19th century stone houses with pitched roofs and plastered facades grouped around the island's protected harbour. Its harmonious sweep is punctuated by two clear verticals–the *campanile* of Aghios Nikolaos and the tall, municipal clock tower; behind the latter is the conspicuous triangular pediment of the Old School Building, set back above the centre of the port. **Emboreió** is an architectural unity created mostly in the 19th and early 20th centuries at the height of the sponge-trade boom which brought considerable wealth to the island.

To the north side of the harbour is the island's principal church of **Aghios Nikolaos**, surrounded by a fine

pebble-mosaic floor (1868), with large and serene cypress-tree and bird designs by the building's east end. Above the apse, high up on the exterior, are capricious relief-decorations of animals. In the forecourt to the south is a baptismal font and the tomb of the church's principal benefactor. Although the church is originally a 16th century foundation, it presents itself today as a largely 19th century re-build; it possesses an impressive *templon*-screen inside. The five-tier **bell-tower** (32m), designed in 1894 by the Rhodian architect, Lefteris Sellas, incorporates pieces of ancient marble from the Temple of Apollo at Pefkiá, two of which form the crown of the arch on the west side. There is a small **ecclesiastical museum** above the narthex, entered from the outside of the church.

Behind the centre of the harbour sweep, stands the **free-standing clock tower** built in the early 1900s by subscription from amongst the island's émigrés in Florida and consciously reflecting the design of the similar clock tower on the harbour-front at Symi—an island with which Chalki had strong links through the sponge-trade. (The clock's mechanism has been stopped and silenced since 1994.) Beside its base, and contiguous with a ruined house to its south, is the still integral, domed chamber of a large **Ottoman cistern** in un-rendered stone, known locally as '*sarantzi*', a corruption of the Turkish *sarnıc* (cistern). Just above, in pseudo-Palladian style, the **Demarcheion** (Town Hall) grandly dominates the skyline; this was also built by émigré subscription, first as a *Lykeion* or school for boys and then later converted into the Town Hall. In front of the steps to the upper floor at the rear of the building are a few ancient marble fragments, including a piece of the lid of a Hellenistic sarcophagus carved with the head of Medusa.

The port extends to the south of the clock tower towards the area originally given over to the sponge-trade. The large stone mansion with blue shutters known as the *Moudouria* (Turkish *müdür*, 'administrator') was the Ottoman governor's office during Turkish occupation. Beyond this, the street leads to the *Hotel Halki* (currently under restoration) which occupies the **old sponge-factory building**. The First World War, followed by restrictions in sponge fishing imposed in 1916 by the Italian occupation, made the sponge industry no longer viable and led to mass emigration by the islanders to Rhodes and—in larger numbers—to Tarpon Springs in Florida where a new and flourishing sponge-trade was built up by the émigré community. It is this community that has financed many of the recent public projects of the island including the newly surfaced road—'Tarpon Springs Boulevard'—completed in 2005 from Emboreió all the way to the monastery of Aghios Ioannis. This road leads west from the port, past the attractive girls' school building of 1914, to a rise at the edge of the town where it splits—right to Kánia Bay (*see below*) and straight on to the interior of the island.

NORTH TO PEFKIA AND KANIA BAY

As the road crosses the low ridge above Emboreió, the left branch beside a wide turning leads to the ruined church of **Aghios Zacharias**. (*Follow the stone wall on the left running uphill, through a gate and then head right, around the corner of the wall which runs across from left to right. Head further right and uphill towards the trees: the church will come into view below and to the right.*) The church appears to have been built on the site of a pagan temple which, in turn, was succeeded by an early Christian place of worship: many elements of these have been incorporated into the construction of the existing church. The present building sits in the north east corner of the foundations of the Early Christian building. Its interior was finely decorated with 14th century wall-paintings which have been removed (1984) to prevent further decay, and are now exhibited in the church of the St Mary of the Castle, or Panaghia tou Kastrou, in Rhodes.

Returning to the junction at the brow of the hill once again, the ruins of what is believed to have been a fortified monastery, referred to locally as '**Kastraki**', are visible on the low summit toward the east. Only the lower courses of the walls are still *in situ* and are made from large, polygonal stone blocks of a period which clearly predates any Christian use of this site. The wide valley which slopes down to the sea at Kánia Bay, though now largely abandoned, was intensively cultivated for grain up until the Second World War. The road ends at the pebble **beach of Kánia**; it is backed by trees and shade, and looks across the water to Rhodes and the islets in between.

On the saddle of the mountain behind, just to the west of the summit marked by a triangulation post, are the remains of the Hellenistic **Sanctuary of Apollo** at Pefkiá—possibly the 'temple' to which Strabo refers in his description (*Geog.* X 488). The temple stood in the lea at the base of the western shoulder of the final summit. (*It is best approached by circumventing the lower perimeter stone-wall of the valley from behind the stand of pine-trees. The rough path passes a huge standing rock in the middle of the valley, then rises up past a conspicuous cave entrance towards the saddle. The saddle itself has been substantially terraced for cultivation. Well in from* *the ridge, at the right-hand corner, in the lea of the bottom of the shoulder of the mountain, are the overgrown ruins of the temple beside a small stone hut.*) Some finely-turned marble columns, bases, drums and other fragments mark the site of the temple. A carved stone basin and a deep cistern lie just to the northeast. A number of the fragments have the style and proportions of Early Christian cutting, and suggest a possible continuity of cult here in Christian times. From the ridge of the saddle on the north side are uninterrupted views towards Symi, Tilos and the Cnidos peninsula.

WEST TO CHORIO AND THE CENTRE OF THE ISLAND

After leaving the houses behind the port, the roadway passes along the inlet of **Pontamos** (10 min. by foot), with a taverna and attractive beach: the low area inland of here is moderately fertile and supports the cultivation of olives and almonds. Several 4th century BC tombs have been excavated here and have yielded a wealth of finds, including some unusual red-figure, sacred drinking-vessels in the form of the heads of Silenus and Hercules, now in the museum in Rhodes. A short distance due north of Pontamos Bay and of the new road, is the small monastery church of the **Aghii Anargyri**, standing beside the former mule-track leading from the port to Chorió: its south wall is mostly constructed of large isodomic blocks from a pagan building of Hellenistic times. After Pontamos the modern road climbs to the west up the lower slopes of Mount Merovigli—an inhospitable rocky scree that was once intensively terraced and is dotted in places by carved niches in the escarpment. At the top of the rise (25 min.) the road levels out: the deserted settlement of Palaio Chorió is to the left, below the castle on the summit; to the right is the cemetery-church of the **Metamorphosis tou Sotiros**, constructed from a number of re-used ancient blocks and with fragments of Hellenistic funerary monuments visible above the door. Above and behind it is a stretch of ancient wall. There are many large 19th century stone sarcophagi in the graveyard around the church.

The remains of *Palaio Chorió stretch up the mountain slope to the south, punctuated by three whitewashed churches. This was the site of both the capital of the island in Classical Antiquity and again in Mediaeval times, when piracy had made coastal habitation untenable: in both periods the strategic value of the protected and hidden site, below a naturally fortified acropolis guarding the whole of the southeast corner of the island, was prized. Remains from the two periods can be clearly distinguished—the irregular masonry of the mediaeval construction contrasting vividly with the perfectly regular, isodomic masonry used in the ancient fortification and embanking walls. The short stretches of ancient wall, lower down on the hill, probably formed terraces supporting larger buildings above.

The path leads up first to the early 14th century church of the **Panaghia** (*if locked, the key may be obtained from the taverna at Pontamos*). The church has clearly been enlarged westwards in three separate campaigns during its long history, and its construction incorporates ancient fragments amongst which is a conspicuous piece of marble cornice with deeply cut dentils, above a window in the exterior north wall. The interior is a graceful, vaulted chamber with pebble floor, decorated in the apse and on the ceiling with relatively well-preserved **wall-paintings** from the mid 1600s, depicting scenes from the *Early Life and Miracles of Christ* (south side) and from the *Passion* and *Resurrection* (north side), together with scenes from the Acathist Hymn (a 6th century hymn of thanksgiving to the Mother of God), and saints in aureoles above. The colours have retained their intensity in many places. The 19th century wooden **iconostasis**, carved in low relief, is of high quality. On the north wall, immediately beside the door, the plaster has been removed in part to reveal the ancient column and eroded Corinthian capital beneath. A path through the gate at the southwest corner of the courtyard leads uphill to another small church with damaged 15th century wall-paintings and a fine ancient marble drum as altar. Running west from its entrance, is a particularly good example of **Hellenistic walling** in perfect courses of regularly rusticated, isodomic masonry. Remains of the ancient settlement become increasingly apparent as you climb: deep, rock-cut cisterns, often with finely shaped mouths; carved rectangular niches; a **fragment of inscribed architrave** (with the name 'ISANDROS IARATEUS', clearly legible); beside it, the base of a statue with holes for the dowels under the feet; and, just before the final climb to the castle entrance, an area in which the rock has been cut like a shelf, with insets and declivities for the fixing of *stelai* or statuary. The entrance of the castle itself is built up on well-preserved, ancient wall-foundations.

The **Castle of the Knights of St John** bears the coat of arms (above and right) of the Order's Grand Master, Pierre d'Aubusson: the fact that this escutcheon does not yet show the cardinal's regalia which was bestowed on d'Aubusson in 1489 suggests a date for the castle's construction between 1476 and 1489, putting it in the same

period as the castle on Symi with which it is strategically
linked. The entrance leads into a roofless guardroom with
cannon embrasures, before a magnificent **ancient doorway**, constructed from ten dressed, monolithic blocks,
which opens into the oblong area of the ruined interior
of the castle. The **finely castellated north wall** of the enceinte, which follows the line of the ancient Hellenistic
walls, is particularly well preserved, with a narrow sentry
walk, central tower (with latrine beside), and rooms built
into the interior face to accommodate inhabitants during periods of siege. The south wall is mostly collapsed
and preserves only the bases of two of its towers. Midway between north and south walls, a deep cistern (probably of ancient origin) with plaster lining is still visible.
The central area is dominated by the form of the roofless
church of **Aghios Nikolaos**, whose remaining walls show
clear evidence of having been reinforced at a later stage.
Although exposed to the elements, areas of the original
wall-paintings of the church are still visible—both some
colourful abstract decoration just above floor-level and,
high up on the south wall, a still legible panel with St
Nicholas steering a rigged boat at sea which relates to a
persistent tradition that the saint stopped on Chalki and
probably explains the prominence given to churches dedicated to him both here and in Emboreió. To the south

the land drops away dramatically to the Trachiá peninsula below with its two shallow anchorages at the isthmus. There is a magnificent **view** from here of the southwest coast of Rhodes, with its two prominent castles. This
look-out post would have afforded the Knights of St John
protection of the main sea-route into Rhodes from Crete
and the west.

THE WEST OF THE ISLAND

The western half of the island is a dramatically rocky
limestone plateau. Although largely uninhabited and un-
cultivated, it is a mass of wild flowers in the early spring.
There is a scattering of isolated chapels and monastery
churches which are now easier to reach with the new
road. (*The road leads all the way to St John 'The Far' which
is a two-and-a-half hour walk from the port. The rugged
coast of this part of the island has few beaches, but there
are deserted, and largely shade-less, pebble coves. Those on
the north coast—**Aréta**, **Aghios Giorgios** and **Dio Yialí**—
are best reached by boat from Emboreió; **Yialí** on the south
coast, can be reached by a 30 minute walk down the track
that descends southwest from Chorió.*)

Beyond Chorió, the road climbs steeply to the north,
shortly passing (right) the chapel of **Aghia Barbara**, built

into the rock face; a little further on is the small **monastery of the Stavros**, focus of a popular island festival each year on 14 September, in which the cross is enshrouded with branches of basil. Higher still, and set on a green ledge in the grey rocky slope of Mount Merovigli a little way to the right of the road, is the **monastery of the Archangel Michael Panormítis**. A new church has been built in front of the original 10th century hermitage chapel which lies just to its east. A dilapidated stone entrance leads into the tiny vaulted interior, which has a pebble floor and the damaged **vestiges of wall-paintings**. There are two layers here: on the south wall, the colourful fragment of a horse's head and the arms of a saint is probably of the 12th century, while the fine traces of a standing saint on the layer below are of the 10th century and of considerable quality. The pitting all over the lower layer was inflicted at the time the second layer was applied, in order to help the new plaster hold to the surface below. The chapel's altar is a re-used pagan altar-block; and just beside the entrance of the chapel are carved marble fragments from an earlier Byzantine church, possibly on this site.

The main road continues to rise steeply again: as it levels off, a rough track leads away to the right beside a ruined windmill to the church of **Aghios Ioannis** ('**The**

Near') and thence down to the picturesque church of
Aghios Giorgios in a small oasis of green behind the bay
of the same name. The main surfaced road continues
west along the undulating, high plateau of the island's
centre: in the valley below to the left, traversed by stone
walls, the base of a large stone tower is visible. The route
affords marvellous views towards Tilos, Symi and the
Turkish mainland. On the left of the road is the isolated
and abandoned chapel of **Aghios Nikitas**, whose vault
is in imminent danger of collapse. There are vestiges of
wall-painting on the interior walls and some ancient
spolia heaped inside. A little further on, the road ends
at the **monastery of Aghios Ioannis Pródromos** ('**The
Far**'), set in the midst of an airy and fertile upland plain.
The open courtyard is bounded on two sides by cells and
punctuated by a large and very venerable, spreading cypress tree: another stands just to the south of the complex. The main church, with a re-laid floor, is simple and
undecorated inside: 100m to its northwest, however, is
the church of the **Panaghia Enniamerítissa** which incorporates material from an Early Christian predecessor. It
has extensive but damaged 14th century **wall-paintings**
inside and a founder's inscription bearing the date 6875
(years since Creation, i.e. 1375).

The road ends at this point; but a one-hour walk

northwest from here to the western extremity of the island leads to the **Kepháli** promontory where, among the ruins of an enceinte of walls and vestiges of an Early Christian basilica, are the remains of an **ancient tower** which surveyed the sea-routes towards Karpathos. The finding also of Neolithic obsidian tools in this area indicates that this lonely promontory is the oldest inhabited area of the island yet to have been discovered. It looks out onto a stretch of sea-water which is the haunt in spring and summer of the elusive Cory's shearwater.

ALIMNIA

The gentler and greener island of Alimniá (also Alimiá) lies about 6km northeast of Chalki, accessible by a 40-minute journey by caïque or water-taxi (*see Practical Information below*). The beautiful and protected **bay of Aghios Giorgios** where boats arrive, bears out the island's ancient name *Eulimnia* ('with good harbours'). Pliny states that there were two harbours—the other being on the island's east coast and referred to by him as *Emporeio*. As you enter the bay of Aghios Giorgios, to the east is the picturesque church of **Aghios Minás**, beside which rise the ruins of the military buildings put up by the Italians during their occupation of the Dodecanese; ahead, amongst the trees behind the beach, was the main settlement clustered around the church of Aghios Giorgios. The tranquil beauty of the bay is at odds with its recent history: during the Second World War this deep harbour was used by German occupying forces as a submarine base. The base was attacked in April 1944 by seven British commandos who were captured, sent to Thessaloniki and executed. The local islanders confessed to having assisted them and were consequently deported. Since the 1960s the island has been uninhabited. In one of the abandoned buildings (formerly a taverna) near the church of **Aghios Giorgios**, pictures of ships and submarines painted by Italian soldiers can still be seen. The church itself stands in a pebbled courtyard surrounded by mature trees: beside the southeast entrance are some ancient *spolia*—amongst which is a fluted, ancient altar. Inside the church, the altar itself comprises an upturned classical column-base. On the rise above the settlement, excavation has uncovered a late Neolithic settlement.

The ruins of a **14th century Hospitaller castle** crown the sharp peak to the north. The ascent up a loose stone scree is not easy as there is no clear path, and takes the best part of an hour; the effort is rewarded by the magnificent views and the interest of the remains. The considerable density of pot-sherds on all of the south slope suggest that this was a substantial settlement in Antiquity, with a fortified acropolis on the summit. Evidence of this ancient fort is clear from a distance, as the solidly built and perfectly drafted rectangular blocks of the **4th century walls** which rise from the natural rock and underpin the mediaeval castle above, come into view. They are particularly impressive along the north side. A deep cistern with dressed stone blocks forming the mouth lies below the southern rock face: this may be the cistern which is specifically mentioned in the original contract of 1366 for the construction of the mediaeval castle, drawn up between a certain Borrello Assanti of Ischia (the lessee) and the Grand Master of the Hospitallers.

The castle can only be entered with difficulty from the east end. Its views over the island itself and of Rhodes are unimpeded; curiously, the only point which is obscured from view by higher land to the southwest is the castle above Chorió on Chalki. It appears that this small fort (it is little more than 80sq. m in area) must have been superseded by d'Aubusson's much larger construction on Chalki a century later, even though both were kept functioning in the 15th century—in effect surveying the same area, yet out of sight from one another.

Goat-grazing has been more limited on Alimniá, permitting a fuller growth of a varied maquis on the island's slopes. Both cultivated olive and dwarf-cedar trees are more abundant here than on Chalki and there is little of the island's surface that does not have some green cover.

PRACTICAL INFORMATION

851 10 Chalki: area 28sq. km; perimeter 34km; resident population 400; max. altitude 593m. **Port Authority**: 22460 45220. **Travel and information**: www. chalki.gr; *Halki Tours* (T. 22460 45281).

ACCESS

By boat: Daily service (90 min.) from Kameiros Skala on Rhodes (dep. 14.30) by caïque (*Nikos Express* or *Nisos Chalki*), with limited capacity for cars; returning daily at 6am from Chalki. Larger ferries stop at Chalki three times weekly on the route between Rhodes (Main Port) and Karpathos, Kasos and eastern Crete. A local water taxi (*Alevandros, T. 22460 45251 or 6944 434.429*) connects Alimniá with Chalki, on request.

LODGING

Places to stay are limited, although slowly increasing. **The Captain's House** hotel (*T. 22460 45201; captainshouse@ath.forthnet. gr*), open generally May–late Oct, is a charming and hospitable home with garden, set back from the harbour a little east of the main church. For longer stays, *Villa Praxithea (*T. 22410 70172 or 6972 427.272; www.villapraxithea. com*), an elegant house on the waterfront sensitively restored by the owner-architect into furnished apartments, is delightful and much to be recommended.

EATING

A number of tavernas by the port serve fresh, locally-caught fish: **Omonia tou Nouri** on the waterfront has excellent spit-roasts and vegetable dishes in addition.

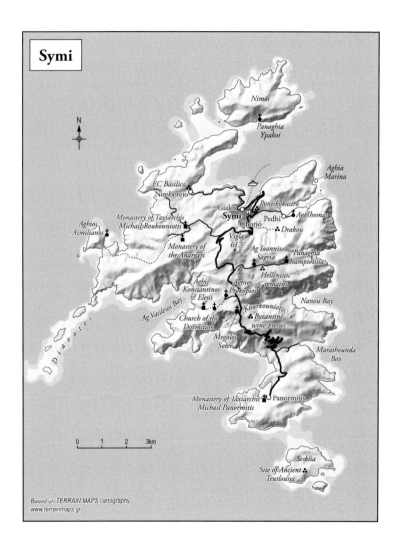

Symi

N

Nimos

Panaghia
Ypakoi

Aghia
Marina

EC Basilica
Nimboreio

Gialos   Pontikokastro
Symi   Ag Thomas
Monastery of Taxiarchis   Pedhi
Michail Roukouniotis   Chorió
Aghios   Drakou
Aimilianos
                  Vigla
Monastery of   617
the Anargyri   Ag Ioannis   Panaghia
                       Sagria   Kampiotissa

                              Hellenistic
Aghii   remains
Konstantinos   Aghios
& Eleni   Prokópios   Nanou Bay
Ag Vasileios Bay   Kourkouniotis
Church of the   Byzantine
Dormition   wine-presses
Megalos   Marathounda
Soter   Bay

Monastery of Taxiarchis Panormitis
Michail Panormitis

0   1   2   3km

Seshlia

Site of Ancient
Teutloussa

Based on TERRAIN MAPS cartography
www.terrainmaps.gr

SYMI

An unusual bargain underpins the recent history of Symi and the impressive beauty of its port which unfolds before the arriving visitor. By maintaining a guaranteed supply of high-quality sponges to the *harem* of the Ottoman Sultan's court, the islanders of Symi gained in return a substantial measure of self-government under the long period of Turkish dominion. They were such talented sailors and renowned shipbuilders that they were also entrusted with making and manning the fast skiffs which carried official post between the *Sublime Porte* and the Ottoman fleet. This was a calculated and realistic compromise on the part of a small Greek community, living on a dry, rocky, infertile island closed in on two sides by the Turkish mainland. It allowed them to continue doing the two things which they did uniquely well: the fishing of sponges and the building of fast boats. As a result, tiny Symi prospered remarkably in the 18th and 19th centuries and became in proportion to its population one of the richest ports of the Aegean: in the process it also became one of the most beautiful, as the harmonious amphitheatre of neoclassical mansions grew and grew around the slopes of its harbour. This was Greek resourcefulness and pragmatism combined at their best.

Today Symi lives by tourism: in the summer the day-trips from Rhodes can seem to engulf the town; but in the evenings and early mornings the island regains its tranquillity and enchantment. A visit to Symi might ideally have three quite different aspects: the leisurely exploration of the harbour and old-town areas; the discovery of the mountainous interior; and a journey by boat around the island's deeply indented coast. The first, which can all be done by foot, would include the stately streets and waterfronts of the port and the old town; the island's two museums—the Nautical Museum for its memorabilia of sponge-fishing practices and ship-building and the Archaeological Museum for its evocation of the island's history and architecture; the castle, built over the ancient acropolis; the churches, many with fine pebble-mosaic forecourts figuring mermaids and sirens; and the houses and grander mansions that line the 'Kali Strata' (the 'fair' or 'beautiful street') which unites the upper and lower towns. Close to this area are the remains of Ancient *Syme*: the imposing, circular, stone podium of '*Pontikó-kastro*', which was probably a victory monument mentioned by Thucydides; the enigmatic remains at '*Drakou*' which may be part of a Hellenistic farm, or possibly a chthonic sanctuary; and the Late Roman or Early Christian mosaics at Nimboreio, found within the remains of an early church. The interior of the island is as rugged as the town is urbane. Sometimes it is just pure rock, sometimes wooded with cedar and fir; it is dotted with painted churches and fortified monasteries. The remains of dozens of Byzantine wine-presses, now ruined, are mute evidence of the island's flourishing trade in wine. But much of Symi can still only be reached by sea: its many pebbled shores with pellucid water and shoreside chapels or monasteries—Aghia Marina, the Panaghia on Nimos, Aghios Aimilianos and, most famous of them all, the monastery of St Michael the Archangel Panormítis, dedicated to one of the most important patron saints of the Aegean world and its mariners. Nor should any boat journey miss, if possible, the uninhabited island of Sesklia, with its shearwaters and seals and shaded shores.

HISTORY AND LEGEND

Symi's mythological origins are variously and conflictingly told by different writers—Diodorus Siculus, Pliny, Eustathius of Thessalonica. It appears that the island cherished a connection with Glaucus whose particular skills associated him with the island's trades—he was a fisherman, sailor and boatwright, and is said to have helped build Jason's ship, the *Argo*. Born mortal, he later became a deity; he abducted Syme, the daughter of king Ialysos of Rhodes, and brought her to the island, endowing it with her name. Ancient *Syme* contributed three ships to the Greek fleet at Troy according to Homer, who says the delegation was captained by the island's young prince, Nereios, who was—after Achilles—the most beautiful warrior amongst the Greeks. Homer relates that he was killed at Troy. Three ships constituted a substantial contingent for a small community which is hardly heard of otherwise in Antiquity and appears never to have minted its own coins. The island's first settlers were allegedly from Caria in Asia Minor; later colonists (11th century BC) were from Laconia, and subsequently from Rhodes and Cnidos. Although the island appears in Athenian tribute lists of 434/3, most of its ancient history from 400 BC onwards is as a dominion of Rhodes. Thucydides briefly mentions the island in his narrative of the naval defeat of the Athenians by the Lacedaimonians off Cnidos in 411 BC. He says the latter set up a trophy on *Syme* to mark their victory: this may correspond to the ancient remains at '*Pontikókastro*' (*see below*).

In Roman and Byzantine times the fate of the island is closely bound with that of Rhodes. Symi appears early on to have begun providing Byzantium with fast ships and good sailors, a service they continued for the Knights of St John after they took the island in 1309. Two Ottoman attacks were successfully repelled in 1457 and 1485; but in 1522, perceiving the futility of further resistance, the island negotiated an agreement with the Turks which guaranteed important concessions of self-governance and free trading, in exchange for certain favours, services and payment of the *maktou* (a fixed, annual, notional tax). Symi could also cultivate land on the Turkish mainland under this agreement. These arrangements ushered in a period of stability and prosperity for the island, in which its sponge-fishing, boat-building and trading all flourished. Theological and religious painting schools of wide repute were established on the island in the 18th century: the painter, Gregory of Symi worked here, and on Tilos and Rhodes. In 1821 Symi revolted and joined with the temporary administration of Independent Greece; but, when in 1830 it was taken under Turkish administration again, its ancient freedoms were severely curtailed. In 1912 the Italians took possession of the Dodecanese from the Turks: Symi's reliance on the fertile lands she held in Asia Minor was cut, her trade collapsed and population declined. In the Second World War the island changed hands several

times. In May 1945 the German surrender of all the Dodecanese Islands was signed on the waterfront at Symi,
and in March 1948 Symi joined the Greek State.

The guide to the island has been divided into two sections
* *The port (Gialós) & the Old Town (Chorió), and their
  vicinity*
* *The interior of the island*

THE PORT (GIALOS) AND THE OLD TOWN (CHORIO)

General layout and appearance

Every approach to Symi by sea runs beside long stretches of rocky and inhospitable cliff: the island seems virtually uninhabited. Then, suddenly, rounding sharply into a long harbour, the steeply rising theatre of coloured, neoclassical houses on all sides comes into view and unfolds—and goes on unfolding. The town seems bigger than expected; and still only a part of it is visible from below. This is just Gialós, the 19th century harbour area; but beyond its high southern ridge it blends continuously into Chorió, the old town of Symi—high up, more ventilated and hidden from the predatory view of passing pirates. The shops, hotels, eateries, cafés and offices are below in Gialós; the museum, the former acropolis, most of the churches and the older houses are in Chorió. A broad staircase of some 500 steps, called the *Kali Strata*, unites the two. It was in effect the main thoroughfare of the town, on which the rich aspired to possess a house. By the water, warehouses lined the cooler north-facing side of the harbour; administrative buildings and the port offices, its south-facing front. At the northwest corner of the inlet, the line of houses draws back, defining a long, open area faced onto by some particularly fine buildings—the Town Hall, the Nautical Museum etc.: this was the old ship-yard and sponge depot, and the commercial heart of Symi. The oddly 'Cotswold-style' stone bridge which cuts this area from the sea was only built in the 1970s, once those activities had long since ceased here. At first a desalination plant was projected for this space; now it has become part *plateia*, part car-park. Ship-building still continues on the island but on a small scale, and is based in the next bay to the north of the harbour.

GIALOS

A pleasantly unreal air is imparted by the symmetry and uniformity of the **houses in Gialós**—most of which date from c. 1830–1910—arranged in a mounting repetition of rectangles and triangles punctuated by pilasters and protruding balconies. The pediments are often characterised by a central circular aperture which allowed air to pass under the roof, cooling the high-ceilinged rooms below. Many of these have now been blocked; some are highly decorative. Characteristic, too, are the thin detached cornices above the windows which keep rainwater on the walls from the window below. A typical large mansion would consist of five levels: a rock cut cistern, at the lowest level; cool rooms for storage at ground or lower ground level; the main floor with entrance and symmetrical plan; the upper floor, with the central balcony, supported on stone volutes, and with wrought-iron railing; and finally the hipped, pedimented roof for ventilation. The **colour** of Symi has undoubtedly changed in recent times. Although strictly controlled by the municipality, the synthetic colours and textures used today (especially a common, custard yellow) are different from the tempera washes used before which were simply pigmented with Attic earth and other iron-oxide colours. These may still be seen on some of the abandoned houses in Chorió: their colours are generally darker and richer. A marine blue was more widely used than today, because of its believed property of averting the evil eye.

The commercial and shopping centre of Gialós is a grid of narrow streets in the area between the end of the harbour and the elegant **Metropolitan Church of Aghios Ioannis Pródromos** (1838). The church stands in an area entirely paved with black and white *chochlakia* (pebble-mosaic) work: it incorporates several ancient fragments found on the site—an inscription in the northwest corner; a curious eroded grave stele by the north door; and part of a draped figure, high up in the north wall. The ornate bell-tower built in marble (with some concrete re-

pairs) stands at the end of a long raised avenue, punctuated by two pairs of exceptional cypress trees, male (as
tall as the bell-tower) and female. In the tower's west face
is the decorated pediment of a Hellenistic marble tomb.
Note also the impressive ship's mast which has been
planted in the forecourt and dedicated here as a votive
offering: this was a frequent practice on Symi and several
other churches in Chorió possess similar trophies. A little way to the north is the open area behind the stone
bridge which was, until World War II, the island's main
boatyard and dry-dock. The dignified and unostentatious
Demarcheion stands on its north side; at the western end
is the **Nautical Museum** (*open daily 11–2.30, summer
only*) in a more extravagant architectural style. It contains
a small collection of memorabilia of the island's maritime
history and of its sponge-divers.

SPONGE DIVING: RICHES TO TRAGEDY

The underwater sloping shores of the Dodecanese
Islands are—or were—a garden for sponges: particularly fertile were the waters of the southern and
western coasts of Symi. In Antiquity these were harvested: there are references to sponges in Book X of
the *Odyssey* and in Aeschylus's *Agamemnon* (l.1329):

Herodotus (VIII.7–8) furthermore tells of the deeds of a certain Scyllias, 'the most accomplished diver of his day'—he is not mentioned as being specifically a sponge-diver, but he is evidence of the primary skill necessary for sponge-diving amongst Ancient Greeks.

The natural abundance of sponges in the waters around Symi and Rhodes and Kalymnos fostered a trade in them from earliest times which was jealously guarded. It was natural that, as the Ottoman Turks increased their grip on the Aegean and its trades in the 16th century, Symi should have sent a preventive deputation to the Sultan in Istanbul in 1522 offering voluntary submission and pleading in exchange for the freedom to continue their skills and trade without hindrance. The deputation brought gifts amongst which were some particularly fine sponges. Suleiman assented; the Symiots succeeded in earning themselves notable freedoms, and amongst the requirements made in return for the freedom of trading in sponges was a yearly tithe of the very finest examples to be sent to the Palace in Istanbul for use in the *Harem*. Symi and her exclusive trade were to prosper enormously on the strength of this agreement as her divers spread out further and further into Ottoman-controlled waters in the Eastern Mediterranean, even as far as the North African coast. Charles Sonnini, writing about the area for Louis XVI at the end of the 18th century, noted that the 'inhabitants of Symi are the most daring and most experienced divers in the world'. The process was slow and dangerous however: the skin divers clung to a perforated diving stone (often a valuable family heirloom) which helped them sink swiftly to the seabed. Two ropes were attached, one to keep the diver in the vicinity of the stone, the other for hauling the stone and the attached net or basket back to the surface afterwards. The diver worked for as long as his lungs would permit—at most three minutes—to cut and basket the sponges in the area of his stone. Then he would loosen himself and swim to the surface, to rest and repeat the process. Others on board would clean, process and store the catch. This laborious and specialised technique meant that sponges remained an expensive luxury item. The nature of the trade also changed the balance of Symiot society: the sponge fleets would leave in the spring, not to return until October. Husbandry and the hard work of the cultivation of the land fell to the women who stayed behind: and not just during the summer, but all through the year, because, as Charles Newton observed as early as 1850, the men made enough money from the season's stock of sponges to consider themselves exempt from anything but leisure during the winter reprieve.

In 1819 the sealed diving suit was invented: this allowed the diver to see clearly underwater, to plumb previously unimaginable depths and to stay below the surface for far longer periods. The diver's yield increased hugely; what was once his skill now became an industrial production. This brought huge wealth to Symi: between 1850 and 1900, the grand houses were built and the town became one of the richest *per capita* in the Aegean. Sponges were exported all over Europe and to America. The divers went down deeper and deeper with ever more sophisticated suits (the *skáphandro*) and, in the process, began to exhaust the sponge-beds. But the tragedy in the end was not primarily that of the sponges, but of the divers. Little was understood as yet of the deleterious effects of deep-water pressure on the human body and, most of all, of the crippling effect of rising too swiftly to the surface. A neurological condition known as Nitrogen Narcosis can set in at depths around 70m and below. Nitrogen traces in the pumped air begin to saturate the blood under pressure; they further compound the problem by forming bubbles in the bloodstream if the ascent through decreasing pressure is not slow and controlled. None of this was properly understood; all that the divers and the sailors saw were the horrid symptoms—the paralysis, the sometimes slow or swift death—that this began to wreak amongst their number. Profit urged them on, in albeit declining numbers, almost until the Second World War, taking what appears to have been an agonising human toll. Today the trade is virtually over in Symi: sponges are now harvested in a different manner, and in different parts of the world—sometimes even by the descendants of Symiot émigrés in Florida or in Australia. Beneath the radiant exterior that Symi presents today it is easy to see the prosperity—harder to sense the tragedy that sponge fishing latterly brought to the island.

A short distance along the north quay of the harbour, known as *Mouraghio*, is a **war memorial** carved into the rock face, which roughly copies the famous *trimolia* relief to Agesander at the foot of the steps to the acropolis of Lindos (*see pp. 199–201*), but bears here an added inscription which reads: '*Today freedom spoke to me secretly. Cease, twelve Islands, from being downcast! 8th May 1945*'. It commemorates the event which took place a little further along the quay in the **Kampsopoulou Mansion** (now the *Hotel Les Catherinettes*) on that date, in which the Germans formally surrendered the Dodecanese Islands to the Allies.

Set back from the seaward end of the *Mouraghio* quay, facing the free-standing clock tower (1881), is the former **Colonial Governorate Building** of the Italian occupation—the only construction on the island in the characteristic and heavily accented, architectural style of Italy's colonies in the Dodecanese during the Fascist period. On the point, just east of here, is a **small bronze statue of a young boy fishing** known as the *Michalaki* ('Little Michael'), by a local Symiot sculptor, Costantinos Balsamis. It is light and whimsical by comparison with Tombros's much heavier, *Unknown Sailor* of 40 years earlier, which is placed in a similar context on Andros.

The road continues into the next inlet of Charani,

dominated by the modern church of the Evangelistria on the hill above and known also as the '*Bay of N.O.S.*' after the acronym for the Symi Naval Club which is further along the shore. This is the area of the present-day **boatyards**. As on Skiathos, in spite of the deforestation of the island which has left the industry without the local source of its primary material, the yards continue a small-scale production at the hands of a number of dedicated artesans. This is all that remains of a millennial tradition of building the finest and fastest boats in the Aegean.

NIMBOREIO

From here a scenic track rounds the headland, with views of the adjacent islet of **Nimos** (Ancient *Hymos*), which has vestigial remains of ancient and mediaeval fortification and habitation, into the tranquil bay of Nimboreió. In the last century Simiots would often keep small houses for the summer here. Nimboreió—as its name implies—was the ancient '*emporeion*' (trading centre) of the island, much later to be superseded by Gialós. The bay has few houses and many churches. Its Early Christian remains lie at the very northern end of the western shore of the bay. (*Beyond the end of the drivable track, continue along the* *narrow pebble shore as far as the last walled enclosure on the water front: from here follow a dried stream-bed inland for 40m. The site is just above, on the left.*) Three contiguous vaulted chapels—dedicated respectively to the Panaghia (the Virgin), the Aghia Kára (the 'Holy Head'), and the Soter[as] (the Saviour)—now occupy what was the panoramic setting of an **Early Christian basilica**; a substantial area of **mosaics** can be seen just to the north of the three chapels. They are dusty and inconspicuous, but a splash of water on them reveals considerable figurative interest—a boy reining in a camel, a goat chasing a roebuck, a *cantharos* flanked by two birds. The subject-matter suggests that these may possibly be from a late Roman villa on this site. The Early Christian church—elements of which are visible in the construction of the central chapel (the oldest of the three)—was later erected over this. The church was probably built in the 6th century; the mosaics may be 150 years earlier. About 50m above and to the south of the churches (where the stand of trees to the left finishes, and almost overlooking the bay) is a hole in the ground which leads into an **underground vaulted catacomb** (locally called the *dodeka spiliá*, '12 caves'), with ten lateral loculi. This may well have been a burial area or possibly the crypt of a now vanished building above, used later as a secret refuge or even as a storage area. Cut masonry for reinforcement directly under this area, can be seen from the shore below.

THE AREA OF CHORIO

There are several routes up from Gialós to Chorió by foot, but the *Kali Strata*, whose broad steps begin just inland of the southwest corner of the harbour, is the most impressive. It passes the finest neoclassical mansions—many ruined, some roofless, some lived-in, some semi-detached (designed as symmetric double habitations), and a few with gardens and venerable trees. Within the limits of the theme, their variety and elegance is remarkable. The summit of the stairs is the beginning of **Ano Chorió**, the Upper Town, which occupies a saddle in the slope of Mount Vigla,which slopes slowly down to the bay of Pedhi to the east, at the end of its fjord-like entrance from the sea. The fertile slope of this valley was the main area of cultivation for the island. The town above spreads around a central eminence topped by the castle (the ancient acropolis). The area immediately around the castle has small, closely clustered houses, narrow stone alleys, and few open spaces. Around the edge of this nucleus are the **earliest neoclassical houses** added at the perimeter of the older area in the early years of the 19th century, before Gialós began to be developed. Here the older tempera colours can be seen on ruined buildings, often—where the plaster is damaged—revealing many layers of different colours, following the various changes in taste and fashion from blue, to red, to yellow. The stone ornamentation and plaster decoration are also more extravagant here than in Gialós.

The museum

(*Open Apr–Oct 8–2.30, closed Mon. Entrance 200m from the main Panormítis road at the top of the inhabited area of Chorió: no access by taxi.*)

The combined **Folklore and Archaeological Museum of Symi** is high up at the southeastern extremity of the town indicated by an (occasionally unreliable) paper-chase of wooden signs through a labyrinth of narrow streets. Housed in two Symiot mansions, the small and informative exhibition area is arranged in half a dozen rooms around a shaded courtyard which contains classical and early Christian fragments, grave-stones and inscriptions. One of the buildings has delightfully painted wooden eaves.

The classical and prehistoric collection in *Room 1* displays several interesting Classical funerary pieces—a fragment of a sepulchral lion, and a shipwrecked sailor's tombstone with characteristic iconography, figuring the naked sailor with his mantle spread on a rock. The Byzantine and early Christian display in *Room 2* has good documentation on the various sites on the island; there is a case of early 13th century Byzantine ceramic bowls with flowing designs of extreme simplicity—remarkable (like those in Kastellorizo's museum) for having survived complete and in such good condition. *Room 3* is dominated by a painted and carved wooden **epitaphios** of great beauty from the Church of Aghios Athanasios, with fine painted scenes of the *Passion of Christ*. This would have been carried around the town once a year in the culminating procession of Holy Saturday. The several examples of 19th century '***mousandra*** **woodwork** in *Room 5* give a good idea of the colourfulness of Symiot interiors—primarily blues and reds, with some green—and the furniture that they contained. Across the courtyard are the house's former service rooms with an exhibit of miscellaneous daily items.

From the edge of the courtyard a stone staircase gives access to the **Chatziagapítos Mansion**. This is an imposing, late 18th century *archontikó* (mansion house) of Italian design—severe and dominating on the outside, but more gracious inside with a colonnaded and pebbled courtyard. The reception rooms are decorated with faded but delightful murals by local artists, and ornately carved wooden panels which are characteristic of the more opulent Symiot interiors.

The Castle

Viewed from the south, the **Castle of the Knights of St John** incorporates a bastion in (massive, but irregular) 5th century BC masonry from the ancient acropolis of Syme, on which once stood a Temple to Athena; abutting it to the left is a semicircular redoubt built by the Knights and bearing the arms of Pierre d'Aubusson as well as the date 1507 which was, in fact, four years after d'Aubusson's death. There are two further redoubts which face east and northeast. These are all later fortifications to the earlier castle of 1407 which remarkably withstood a siege by Mehmet the Conqueror in 1457. On the summit stands the church of the **Panaghia tou Kastrou** (the 'Greater'—so as to distinguish it from the 'Lesser' below): this church was originally dedicated to Aghios Giorgios, but it took the name of the original Panaghia church to the south after that was destroyed by German forces in 1944. To right and left of the entrance door are Hospitaller escutcheons in stone, taken from the walls of the castle. Inside the church is the renowned and beautiful **icon of the Second Coming** by the late 16th century Cretan artist, Giorgios Klontzas. To one side of the church's belfry hangs an anomalous bell made from the nose of an enemy bomb. Around the perimeter of the area cluster two other small chapels; that on the north has a small (recent) mural, and a painted *prothesis* niche whch would seem to indicate that it was perhaps once more fully decorated with painting. Although, from the Hospitallers' point of view, the castle was not especially practical for signalling purposes, the **panorama** from its heights is spectacular, including in its sweep the coast of Asia Minor, Gialós, the bay of Pedhi and the ridge in between with its line of windmills which culminate in some unusual ancient remains, towards which this itinerary is now directed.

Below the castle, to the east, is the **church of the Panaghia Katomeniá** (the 'Lesser' or 'Lower'). Its interior is modern but contains a finely carved iconostasis, throne, pulpit and lectern; although gilded and painted, these have much greater lightness because they are not varnished. Further to the northeast is the (now superannuated) **Old Pharmacy** building—a memorable piece of Symiot neoclassical architecture, complete with 19th century fitments in the interior and a makeshift operating room behind. Together with the creation of the public 'Reading Rooms' in Gialós and Chorió, this is an expression of the keen municipal civic-sense which characterised late 19th century Symi.

'PONTIKOKASTRO'

On the ridge of the hill (called 'Noulia') to the northeast of Chorió is a line of more than 15 **windmills** in varying states of decay, which once produced the rough flour used for Symi's famous breads and for the biscuits which were the staple of the island's mariners while at sea. Beyond them, and just above, is an enigmatic ancient construction known as the *Pontikókastro*—a circular drum of massive, roughly finished, ashlar masonry. Seventeen metres in diameter, and on average about 1.5m high, it has the masonry typical of the 5th century BC. A few metres to the west of it, is a slightly flattened rectangular stone area which may be related to it. In the *Peloponnesian War* (Book VIII, 42) Thucydides mentions that the Spartans and their allies, after their naval victory over the Athenians off Cnidos in 411 BC, 'sailed with combined fleet to Syme and *there set up a trophy*, and anchored again at Cnidos'. A construction at this particular point makes no clear sense as a defensive or look-out post because its view is too restricted. More plausible is the idea that this massive, circular platform should be the base for a victory monument displaying the spoils of battle, such as that mentioned by Thucydides.

THE '*DRAKOU*' ARCHAEOLOGICAL SITE AND PEDHI BAY

To the east of *Pontikókastro* and of Chorió, the fertile valley behind Pedhi Bay descends gently to the sea. On the lower slope of the steep hills that form the south side of this valley is another archaeological curiosity, referred to by its popular local name '**Drakou**' ('dragon's lair'). (*Sited half way up the southern slope of the valley and level with a line about 100m back from the shore. Not easy to find. Access by the rough track (signed) leading east from the first hairpin bend after the habitation of Chorió ends on the Panormítis road. 20 min. by foot*). There are two elements here, both ancient: an unidentified but very cleanly constructed **edifice in ashlar masonry**; and an area of walling, terracing or **fortification**, just beyond (east) and further up the hill. The latter has been modified by mediaeval and later walling in small irregular stones which has been raised up on top of it. The former—a building of uncertain purpose—is more remarkable because of the very fine cutting and finishing of it large limestone elements. Earth has filled so much of the area that it is difficult to get a sense of the whole. What is visible consists of two chambers: one larger, sunk in the ground, and one smaller, above it to the south. The south door of the main chamber is beautifully finished and mounted. On the north wall are two curious, deep rectangular indentations: the whole area is scattered with cleanly cut blocks with architectural elements—protrusions and recesses. The precision with which they are worked would suggest a 4th century BC date for the masonry. Although the building's unusual form, with its sunken elements, overlooking virtually the only fertile area of the island and facing east, brings to mind a place for the cult of Demeter, more plausibly these remains belong to a large, secular building relating to the agricultural work of the valley. The wider area has yielded evidence of Late Bronze Age settlement.

Pedhi Bay

The attractive bay of Pedhi, frequented by Simiots once as a summer 'retreat', has a beautiful setting and a number of fine houses. At the south end of the bay is a concentration of older churches. Behind the first row of houses from the shore-line just before the bay bends east is the 15th cen-

tury church of the **Taxiarchis Michail Avlakiotis** (paintings in poor condition on the north wall). The most interesting church in the area is **Aghios Thomás**, which lies
100m along the south shore from the corner of the bay.
It is set back a few feet from the sea, and between it and
the shore is an enclosed area where fresh water springs
emerge from under the church, creating a pool to the
side, in which fish seem to delight. The pool has an apse
to the east and a number of ancient stones in the water
which come from an early Christian church which once
stood here, and for which the springs may have served for
baptisms. This in turn may have replaced an earlier pagan
shrine on the same site.

From Pedhi Bay, local boats can be hired to go to the
islet of **Aghia Marina** which lies just off the coast to the
north of the entrance to the bay. There is a tiny monastery beside the water. It is also swimming-distance from
the coast opposite, where there is a small seasonal community which can be reached by foot (30 min.) from the
north side of Pedhi Bay.

THE INTERIOR AND THE NORTH OF THE ISLAND

The island is traversed from north to south by a 24km, metalled road that runs from Gialós to Panormítis. Most sites and points of interest can be explored by small diversions or walks off this main axis. Some of the coastal sites of the island are more easily reached by local boats from the harbour, however; this is indicated in the text where relevant. The route crosses the high plateau of the interior and gives a good sense of the variety of the island's terrain.

TO THE WEST

Climbing steeply up from the edge of Chorió, the road passes the town's cemetery at **Aghia Marina**. In 1765 an important library and school of religious studies, theology and painting was founded here which flourished for nearly 60 years. At 7km, after reaching a panoramic altitude, a junction is signed (right) to the **monastery of the Taxiarchis Michail Roukouniotis** (4km) whose entrance is marked by a walled enclosure around a spreading cypress tree of majestic dimensions. Although the monastery is no longer functioning, it is cared for and kept open by a local guardian. The foundation is probably 11th century, although the gate-way and much of the monastic building which surrounds the *catholicon* date from an 18th century rebuilding. Like many other Symiot monasteries, it is built four-square, like a fortress. The space inside tightly encloses the *catholicon* which has two levels: the lower level, almost like a subterranean grotto, has paintings (now very blackened) and a pebble floor; in its tiny domed narthex are original traces of the *Four Evangelists* in the squinches; the upper level, rebuilt after a fire in the 14th century, is decorated with **murals** by the island's best known painter, **Gregory of Symi**, in a popular, narrative style (1738). There appears to have been an Early Christian building on this site (witness the upturned capital just inside the entrance gate). The monastery, which was latterly under Russian protection, possessed from early times an important library; a 12th century Gospel was rescued from the fire here and is now in Rhodes. Passing on the track below the monastery along the edge of a military camp, you soon come to the **monastery of the Anargyri** (visible just across the valley), decorated similarly with 18th century wall-paintings.

From here, a meandering track (1 hr) leads west to the secluded *bay of Aghios Aimilianos, where a tiny church and monastery sits on an islet joined to the shore by a causeway. This may also be reached by boat (45 min.) from Gialós. Constructed in the mid 19th century by the Hadjimichalis family, the monastery is typical of many that were built by rich families and donated to the Church, whose right it was to choose the dedication; the family would often endow the building for its future maintenance and would be able to use it for retreat at their discretion. The monastery is symmetrical, with two residential blocks to either side (able to accommodate 12 monks) and an arcade on the lower level, surrounding a low undecorated chapel. Between the entrance and the causeway is the inconspicuous grave of a 16 year-old girl from Kalymnos who was killed here in 1942. The attractive setting between the sea and the mountains is unforgettable.

TO THE EAST

The main north/south road continues towards Panormítis, passing a turning for the Panaghia Stilou (8km). Shortly after, the monastery of **Aghios Konstantinos** (which has 19th century wall-paintings) is on the left, while across the valley from it, the clear, raised, serpentine line of the former flagstone road is visible winding up the opposite slope to the west. At 11km, a narrow road is signed left to Chames and Kampiotissa and descends rapidly into an inhospitably rocky landscape. By following this turning you come at the top of the subsequent rise to the 13th century church of **Aghios Ioannis Prodromos Sagriá** marked by two large ilex trees: its interior has paintings in poor condition. Just beyond and around the corner, on the rise to the right of the road, are clear signs of ancient construction, probably the base of what was an impressively large **Hellenistic fortified building**. There has been some later building on top—a shepherd's house, winnowing areas, etc.—but the lower level shows a clear rectangular base with finely interlocked blocks, best preserved on the west, north and east sides. The position dominates the whole valley. On the top of the peak to the east of here are the remains of a mediaeval fort. A kilometre and a half further down this road (past impressively folded rock-formations to the left) is the small nunnery of the **Panaghia Kampiótissa** (no longer functioning). This is a remote and peaceful place: the small vaulted chapel has a venerable carved door, and an inlaid stone floor.

THE AGHIOS PROKOPIOS VALLEY

Just beyond the Chames/Kampiotissa junction, the road reaches its summit (12km) and then slowly descends. At 13km, an alluvial dip in the rocky landscape forms a tiny fertile circular plain for cultivation, appropriately called *Xerolimniá* ('dry lake'). Here a track (signed) to the right leads towards the isolated church of **Aghios Prokopios** with 15th century wall-paintings, set in a densely wooded valley full of birdsong. On the south side of the valley, and visible on the crest of the hill from below, are **two small monasteries** reached by means of a delightful and shaded walk that climbs up through the woods. The nearest, dedicated to the **Koímisis tis Theotókou** (Dormition of the Virgin), is a walled enclosure with two parallel churches inside, not visible from the outside. The church to the north is recent; the other is of the 16th or 17th century, with an inlaid stone floor and amply decorated with **wall-paintings** in the upper area that maintain much colour and clear definition. These have been subjected to over-cleaning which has left the colour-tone without depth, but they give a clear idea of the vivacity and narrative strength of the school of Symiot painters of the 18th century, to whom these should be attributed. Even the rib of the vault has been beautifully decorated on all three of its facets. The enclosure is marked externally to east and to west by two monumental ilex trees, which have managed in this rocky terrain to find sufficient water to grow to a remarkable size. By the western tree, a steep path leads on up to the west towards the **monastery of Aghii Kon-**

stantinos and Eleni, sitting on a ridge which commands unbeatable **views** of the east and north of the island, and of the Cnidos peninsula across the water in Turkey. To the east below the main enclosure, is the older chapel of the Aghii Anargyri.

Continuing on the main road in the direction of Panormítis, after 200m from the Aghios Prokopios turn is the wayside chapel of the Panaghia which has a small mural of the Madonna and Child Enthroned. A further 200m on is **Aghia Marina**, also to the right of the road but more hidden in the trees, where an unexpectedly imposing and wide-eyed *Christ Pantocrator* fills the tiny apse of the church, and paintings cover the vault. These are substantially earlier (15th/16th century) and have a more dramatic style than the urbane murals at the church of the Koímisis, mentioned above. Another 200m further south on the road is the monastery of the **Megalos Soter** (the Saviour). This is an 18th century foundation with contemporaneous wall-paintings by artists of the local school.

To the east of here (across the road from the Megalos Soter), a broad and moderately fertile valley slopes down into a ring of hills. On the eastern peak are visible the remains of a mediaeval castle; the valley is criss-crossed with walls and terraces which have been constantly rebuilt, but whose material and lines are Byzantine in origin; in the centre of the lower level of the valley a tiny church—now mostly whitewashed inside—still preserves a small, 15th century painted fragment of the **Madonna and Child Enthroned** of surprising beauty and elegance. The area is known as 'Kourkouniotis', and by virtue of being hidden from the sea and more fertile than most of the island, it appears to have been lived in and cultivated since Neolithic times. It is uninhabited now and most of what is visible today dates from the 11th to 17th centuries. The most remarkable remains here are of a large number of **Byzantine stone wine-presses** scattered all over the southern slopes of the valley amongst the cypress and fir trees. (*Take the path which follows the contour of the hill, just below the level of the asphalt road for about 700–800m. On a leisurely reconnaissance, at least two dozen can be seen.*)

BYZANTINE STONE WINE-PRESSES

These are different from the rock-cut wine-presses found on Kastellorizo which are ancient and more than a thousand years older: but the habit of cultivating and pressing wine on Symi in Byzantine times probably follows directly on from ancient cultivation and wine-production in the same places before. Unlike the presses of Kastellorizo these Byzantine presses are built up from the ground, and although most were open cylindrical structures, some were closed by a corbelled roof. A few have been partially restored. The site of a press was determined first by locating a natural, sloping patch of limestone in the ground, which had a smooth and eroded surface. On this base a ring of large vertical stone-slabs was built which created an impermeable circle (generally a little over 2m in diameter) which contained the harvested grapes, and allowed two people to tread and press them, working face to face and holding one another's shoulders. Around this circle a small tower was raised in smaller stones which took the overall height up further—generally to about 1.5m, but sometimes to as much as 2m if the press were roofed. At the lowest point of the sloping stone floor is an emissary to allow the juice to drain out into a stone basin or channel outside the press. The emissary probably had a simple improvised filter, woven from dried broom. At Kourkouniotis, the presses are built high up on a steep incline above the area where the vines grew. This must have been inconvenient for the transportation of both the grapes and the wine produced; but the natural rocks that formed the floors had to dictate the whereabouts of the presses. Although such presses are found in greatest concentration in the area of Kourkouniotis, they occur in several other locations on the island, and different areas present different styles of construction. A number of early visitors to Symi particularly praise the quality of its white wine, amongst them Cristoforo Buondelmonti who visited in 1420 and noted that 'the island produces exceptional wine'. Symi's commerce in wine was obviously significant in Byzantine times: then came the Islamic, Turkish occupation of the Asia Minor mainland, and her market rapidly diminished. By 1600 production was virtually only for local consumption, and the presses fell into disuse.

The final stretch of the road to Panormítis, descends dramatically down to sea-level again, with sweeping **views** of the southern tip of the island and towards Tilos, Chalki and Rhodes. Below, the almost perfect ellipse of the cove of Panormítis with the monastery on the south shore, comes into view. At 22km a turning to the east (left) leads down to the pebble beach of **Marathounda** in a peaceful and enclosed bay and creek. At 24km, the road ends at the ***monastery of the Taxiarchis Michaïl Panormítis** whose extensive buildings stretch along the protected and embracing waterfront with the pine-clad hills behind. (*Open 7–2 & 4–8, every day. Appropriate dress required. Simple accommodation (T. 22460 71354) can be obtained in the monastery buildings, although reservation is advisable from July–Sept. There are direct boat connections from here to Rhodes in summer.*) The long block of 19th/20th century buildings which overwhelm the small church at their centre, are designed to accommodate the large numbers of pilgrims and sojourners who gather here in the summer months and for the saint's festival (7–9 November). There is a shop, bakery and taverna. The surprising size of the complex can be explained by the profound importance of the cult of the Archangel Michael both in the islands in general and on Symi.

THE ARCHANGEL MICHAEL

In the Eastern Orthodox Church, St Michael is widely accorded greater importance and veneration than he is in the Western Church. For several reasons, in the Greek Islands his protection is especially invoked: and in few places more than here on the island of Symi, of which he is the patron saint. The American Negro spiritual song, 'Michael, row the boat ashore!', is a reminiscence of the ancient tradition that he was the receiver of the souls of the dead: in many icons (as here in this monastery) he holds a tiny swathed human soul in his left hand and his drawn sword in his right hand. But the 'rowing of the boat', also records his solidarity with, and special protection of, all sailors and ships: hence his particular importance in the sea-girt world of the Greek Islands. Always seen armed and ready for action, he is more generally the captain of the Heavenly Host (*Revelation*, XII, 7), and patron of the Christian militant cause and of its soldiers. Again this gave him further importance on Christianity's frontier with Islam in the Aegean during the late Middle Ages and after. For all the above reasons, the choice of St Michael as the supreme protector of Symi is not a surprise. In the Eastern Church, Michael is also the protector of the sick, and for this reason his shrines are crowded with votive gifts not just from mariners and soldiers but also from the cured and the sick. Here, as 'Panormítis' ('of the place where there is always anchorage'), his veneration replaces an earlier pagan cult of Poseidon, the ancient protector of mariners, over whose temple the monastery's church is allegedly built. Mariners in Antiquity took care to honour the divinity of Poseidon before undertaking any voyage. Here, on Symi, the sponge-fishing fleets would always come round from Gialós harbour to Panormítis for special blessing before they left for their often dangerous months at sea in the Eastern Mediterranean.

The improbable three-tier **bell-tower** built in 1905 over the central gate, complete with affixed terracotta eagles and *acroteria*, gives onto an **arcaded courtyard** paved with abstract pebble mosaics which surrounds the plain exterior of the *catholicon* in the centre. The latter was rebuilt completely in 1783 (inscription on façade) by Anastasis Karnavas from Rhodes, replacing an earlier monastery here of which there are notices only as far back as 1460, but which may well have been a 5th or 6th century foundation in origin. The **interior** of the *catholicon* is dark and impressively decorated. It is a single nave, with 'gothic' cross-vaulting in a typical Dodecanesian style, entirely decorated with **wall-paintings** by the Symiot brothers **Nikitas and Michail Karakostides** (inscription over entrance) in 1792. They are in relatively good condition, best preserved on the north side. Allowing even for cleaning, it appears that the blue used here is not the dark indigo blue of Constantinopolitan painting but a locally preferred, paler hue. The massive, walnut-wood **iconostasis** by **Maestro Diakos Tagliaduro of Kos** (whose two other known works are in Jerusalem and Russia) is a monument of virtuoso carving. Note, for example, the twisted Solomonic columns which have vines carved all around them in relief and delicately wrought birds which stand out even from the vines. To the right-hand side is the icon of the Archangel (1724), armed in silver and precious stones, and surrounded by an ever-renewing mass of *ex votos*.

The monastery has two museums (*combined entrance ticket*)—an Ecclesiastical Museum and a Folklore Museum—as well as a library and picture gallery. Between them these contain a remarkably varied range of ecclesiastical objects, icons, furniture and votive gifts—amongst them ceramics, ivory, stuffed animals, fine models of ships, and countless bottles containing donations or prayers to Saint Michael, which were launched on the waves in different parts of Greece and by one route or another have found there way here to Panormítis. There are memorabilia also to the brave and ultimately tragic resistance organised from the monastery during the Second World War when Allied soldiers were given sanctuary here and a radio-signal transmitter was set up: these acts cost the abbot, Fr. Chrysanthos Maroudakis, and two of his local helpers, their lives when they were executed in front of the monastery in February 1944 by German forces. A room in the museum and a monument on the promenade, commemorate this. In 1945 the monastery was a staging post for refugees returning from Turkey. After the war ended, it was in parlous state and virtually abandoned: for the next three decades, it was laboriously taken in hand and rebuilt under the organisation of a single monk who, having made a vow to St Michael when the ship in which he and his family were travelling was torpedoed and sunk, dutifully gave the rest of his life and energy to the monastery in gratitude to the Archangel for his miraculous survival.

SESKLIA

Sesklia, the small island south of the southern tip of Symi, belongs to the Monastery of Panormítis. In common with many of Symi's surrounding islands and the sheltered bays around its perimeter, there is archaeological evidence of human presence as far back as the late Neolithic period (4th millennium BC). Sesklia's ancient settlement was named '*Teutloussa*'. There are small stretches of its ancient wall near the island's summit. Thucydides mentions in his *Peloponnesian War* (VIII.42) that it was here that the Athenian fleet under its general, Charminos, retreated and hid after its unexpected defeat at the hands of Spartan ships off Cnidos in 411 BC. The island has some beautiful shoreline for swimming and is surprisingly green, with a variety of vegetation supporting a vigorous bird life—including partridge which in turn attracts raptors. Cory's shearwater also breeds here, and can been seen gliding and fishing in the open waters between here and Karpathos.

PRACTICAL INFORMATION

856 00 Symi: area 57sq. km; perimeter 88km; resident population 2594; max. altitude 617m. **Port Authority**: 22460 71205. **Travel and Information**: 22460 71397, www.symi-island.com

ACCESS

The island has no airport, and only three or four ferry services a week from Piraeus (16 hrs). Access is easy from Rhodes, however, where there is a selection of fast daily (c. 1 hr) services by hydrofoil (*Aigli*), and catamaran (*Dodekanisos Express*), or by regular ferry (*Symi I and II*): these are all managed by *ANES Co., T. (Rhodes) 22410 37769; (Symi) 22460 71444. F/B Kalymnos* runs local routes to Kos, Kalymnos, Astypalaia, Rhodes and Kastellorizo, once a week.

LODGING

Historic, with painted ceilings and delightful views from the rooms, the **Hotel Les Catherinettes** (*T. 22460 72698 & 71671*) on the north waterfront of the harbour (close to where the ferries dock) is not expensive, but the comfort is basic and the balconied rooms can be noisy at night. **Garden Studios** (*T. 22460 72429*)—quiet, in a Symiot house surrounded by a garden—are set some way back from the southwest corner of the harbour; just beyond this, **Opera House Hotel** is similar in concept, but is larger and less intimate (*T. 22460 72035*). Both have comfortable studio apartments at moderate price. More expensive and stylish is the **Hotel Aliki** (*Apr–Oct only*) in a restored mansion on the south waterfront (*T. 22460 71655*), with a pleasant roof-terrace. Monastic lodgings can be arranged at the **Monastery of Panormítis** in the south of the island (*T. 22460 71354*).

EATING

On the south waterfront of Gialós are two good eateries of quite different character: **Mythos** serves ambitious variants on traditional Greek dishes—mostly imaginative and successful (especially with simple ingredients such as courgettes and aubergines): both chef and wine-list are acclaimed. Further out along the same waterfront is **Dimitri,** for those seeking a simple, unostentatious *mezedopoleion*, serving fresh fish mezes, expressly prepared. Similar in style, **Meraklis** (set back from the port near the Metropolitan Church of Aghios Ioannis) has good home-cooked dishes that are less specifically fish-oriented.

FURTHER READING

William Travis, *Bus Stop Symi*, Readers Union, Newton Abbot, 1973.

INDEX

Nigel McGilchrist is an art historian who has lived in the Mediterranean—Italy, Greece and Turkey—for over 30 years, working for a period for the Italian Ministry of Arts and then for six years as Director of the Anglo-Italian Institute in Rome. He has taught at the University of Rome, for the University of Massachusetts, and was for seven years Dean of European Studies for a consortium of American universities. He lectures widely in art and archaeology at museums and institutions in Europe and the United States, and lives near Orvieto.